The Secret of Positive Praying

The
Secret
of
Positive
Praying

JOHN BISAGNO

PYRANEE
BOOKS

Zondervan Publishing House
Grand Rapids, Michigan

The Secret of Positive Praying
Copyright © 1986 by The Zondervan Corporation
Grand Rapids, Michigan

Pyranee Books is an imprint of Zondervan Publishing House,
1415 Lake Drive, S.E., Grand Rapids, Michigan 49506.

Library of Congress Cataloging in Publication Data

Bisagno, John R.
    The secret of positive praying.

    "Pyranee books."
    1. Prayer. 1. Title.
BV210.2.B568   1986   248.3'2   85-31474
ISBN 0-310-21152-2

Unless otherwise indicated, Scripture quotations are from the King James
Version of the Bible.

Printed in the United States of America

86 87 88 89 90 91 / 10 9 8 7 6 5 4 3 2

Contents

Preface

Many of you will be familiar with my earlier work, *The Power of Positive Praying*. With deep gratitude to our Lord for His blessing upon that book, I would like to share with my readers a few thoughts regarding this sequel, *The Secret of Positive Praying*. Hundreds of thousands of persons have bought and read *The Power of Positive Praying*. Innumerable letters have come in with accounts of schools and Bible study groups using the author's humble efforts upon those pages as a teaching guide to prayer. With great gladness of heart I thank God that it has been a blessing to so many. That book was a purposeful effort to instruct the layman in how to pray.

Many of my readers have been gracious enough to request additional insight into prayer. How many times have I made the comment, half in jest and half in sincerity, "Being only twenty-five years of age when I wrote that book, I look back today at fifty and admit I didn't know I knew that"? Surely God had something to do with helping me to write those earlier pages. Now, after the continued spiritual growth of two decades, it is my humble prayer that these pages might augment our earlier effort with a broadening river of spiritual insight to our readers. That you have been blessed by Part I is a great delight. That you may be blessed by *The Secret of Positive Praying* is my sincere prayer for all who journey with us through these pages. Moody once heard it said, "The world has yet to see what God can do with one man completely surrendered to His purpose."

"By God's grace," said Moody, "I'll be that man." Equally might it be said, "The world has yet to see what God can do through the power of positive praying."

No prayer means no power. Little prayer means little power. And much prayer means much power. Our world is in desperate need of that which only our Lord can do, and prayer is the force that moves the hand of God. To what greater cause could we commit ourselves as the body of Christ than to a massive effort in world-wide prayer for ourselves and for our world. It is our sincere prayer that the humble effort of this new work may have some small part in bringing to pass just such a revival of world-wide prayer power.

Part I

Promises of Prayer

CHAPTER 1

The Secret of Positive Praying

By "praying positively" we simply mean that believing God will answer our prayer is the essential ingredient in evoking a positive response from heaven. Far too often our prayers are no more than a "shot in the dark"—a kind of sanctified, wishful thinking, as evidenced by our complete surprise when prayer is occasionally answered. "Without faith it is impossible to please God."

But it is essential to keep in focus that while He promises "All things are possible to them that believe" and "Whatsoever ye ask in my name, that will I do" and "According to your faith so be it," our Lord has been gracious enough to provide a "heavenly governor" to keep us from praying outside of His will. Far too often our well-intended prayers are foolish at best. One of the most important lessons I have learned during the last twenty-five years is to thank God that He didn't answer all my prayers!

The promises of God which appear to give us a blanket guarantee to answer our prayers for any and all things are fortunately hedged by a second provision—that we pray in accordance with His will and in His name.

Bible names were very important as a reflection of the

sum total of the character, personality, and achievements of a person. "In His name," then, means the sum total of all He is and wills. What Jesus "is," does not exist separately from what He "wills." His desire, His purpose, His will is tantamount to the Lord Himself. One cannot serve Him and claim His power and blessings apart from service in harmony with what He desires. The expression "In His name," then, becomes synonymous with the expression "In His will." We ought to be thankful that He provided this heavenly governor to counterbalance the seeming open-ended promise to grant us whatever we ask. What "we will," then, must be in harmony with what "He wills."

The secret to answered prayer is not simply assuming a guarantee to answered prayer by tossing in the expression, "In His name." Nor is answered prayer simply on the basis of adding, "If it be Thy will," to our prayers. This expression far too often indicates we really have no faith at all and that we are actually saying, "If you were going to do it anyway, then go ahead and do it." But "Thy will be done" praying was never intended to be a fine-print escape clause to get us off the hook when nothing happens in answer to our prayers. And that kind of praying generally guarantees that nothing will happen.

The two ingredients that must be in any prayer for God to act, then, are (1) God's willingness to bestow; and (2) my faith to believe. And both ingredients are essential to answered prayer. Someone will ask, "But if it is God's will, then won't it happen anyway?" The answer to that question is a resounding No! God's will is not always done. It is not His will that men rebel, sin, die, and perish, but man has a will of his own. The very fact that God loved man enough to give him the capacity to choose to serve Him necessitates the accompanying capacity to choose to reject Him. God's perfect will shall ultimately be done, but God's permissive will currently allows for willful man to create a hell-on-earth that was never within the perfect will of God.

Let it be clearly stated, then, that the will of God is not always done. Many things, in fact most things, that exist in this world today are not in the will of God. Satan himself is the Prince of Power in this age. One day our Absentee Landlord will come and take back that which is His own; but that day is not yet. So remember that just because something is God's will does not necessarily mean it will be done. For God to act, a thing must first of all be in His will, but must also include my faith to receive it.

We are to be cautioned on two points. Just because something is God's will does not necessarily mean it will come to pass unless I believe that it will happen. Conversely, just because I believe something will happen, in no way assures that it will happen unless it lies within the will of God. Let it be clearly stated again, then, that two things are necessary for God to act in answer to prayer—*God's willingness to bestow* and *my faith to believe.*

Two important truths must be in focus for the believer who would take seriously the joint cooperation of these two precepts in moving the mighty hand of God through prayer. The first is learning to discover His will; the second, learning to believe Him with great faith.

In attempting to learn His will, several truths will greatly aid us.

1. *God is more willing for you to know His will than you are to know it.* God is not playing cat-and-mouse with you. He is not trying to hide His will or keep it from you. He is making every effort to reveal it to you.

2. *God promises to give guidance, but not always in advance.* Sufficient light for today is given, for that is all that is required. As we step by faith into the light we do have, He gives more light.

3. *His will is not always immediately pleasant.* Romans 8:28 promises,

13

> And we know that all things work together for good to
> them that love God, to them who are the called
> according to His purpose.

The promise is not that all things are good, for some things
are bad. The promise is that the good and the bad interact
to produce the best.

4. *Assistance in knowing His will when coming through
another will usually come unsolicited.*

5. *Essential to knowing His will is being willing in
advance to know it.* You cannot ask God to reveal His will
to you in order to learn whether or not it is something you
want to do. You must pray, "Thy will be done," and mean
it in order to learn His will. Often God does not want us to
do some unpleasant thing, but simply wants us to be
willing to do anything that we might learn to trust Him.
Thereby, we become worthy of knowing and then doing
His perfect will.

6. *God reveals His will to us through circumstances.* Open and closed doors may be viewed as answers
from God when the heart is sincerely praying, "Show me
Thy will."

7. *God gives guidance through His Word.* Where the
Bible gives specific direction, His will is clear. More often,
however, the Bible deals in concepts and principles.
Reading His Word creates a spiritual sensitivity such that
the knowledge of His will comes easily to us.

8. *The "still small voice of God" speaks His will to us in
most cases with a kind of "holy hunch."* Most often we know
His will through the deep-seated impression that just will
not go away. The heart, the emotions, the conscience,
indeed are to be trusted if we are sincerely asking for His
guidance. It is absolutely imperative that you learn this
great principle. *The way God answers your prayer for specific
directions in His will is by putting the desire in your heart to do*

His will. To the sincere Spirit-filled believer consistently seeking the will of God, the answer to the question, "What does God want me to do?" may simply be stated, "What do you want to do?"

The second ingredient in answered prayer is "our faith to believe." We must first learn His will and then understand that just because it is His will, it will not automatically come to pass. There *must* be added to "His willingness to bestow," "my faith to believe." Faith may be built by praying bite-sized prayers, believing God for the little things that we might step up gradually to learn to believe Him for the big things. Faith comes by hearing the Word of God. Faith comes by approximating ourselves to regular worship with the company of believers. But *few* things build faith like *time* in prayer. To learn to trust someone I must take time to know them. This includes time in praise, thanksgiving, confession, petition, intercession, waiting for God to speak to me in the "still small voice," and offering my prayer "in His name" and "in His will."

But perhaps no more important ingredient may be seen in building our faith than a clear understanding of what faith truly is.

> Now faith is the substance of things hoped for, the evidence of things not seen. *Hebrews 11:1*

In Paul's grand statement on faith he is saying that faith has substance and reality. It acts and does and accomplishes because it believes God and takes Him at His word. *Faith is being willing to stretch higher than you can reach.* Faith is being willing to risk, to dare, to dream. Faith is not believing God *can,* it is believing God *will.* And that, even now, it is as good as done.

CHAPTER 2

Our Privilege in Prayer

God has given man no higher privilege than that of communion with Himself. The Scriptures are replete with promises and encouragement in prayer.

> Confess your faults one to another, and pray one for another, that ye may be healed. The effectual fervent prayer of a righteous man availeth much. *James 5:16*

> And it shall come to pass, that before they call, I will answer; and while they are yet speaking, I will hear. *Isaiah 65:24*

> And whatsoever ye shall ask in my name, that will I do, that the Father may be glorified in the Son. If ye shall ask anything in my name, I will do it. *John 14:13–14*

> Call unto me, and I will answer thee, and show thee great and mighty things, which thou knowest not. *Jeremiah 33:3*

Time would forbid to tell of earth's heroes in prayer. The pages of history are filled with the miraculous movings of the Spirit, occasioned by the praying of such men as Joseph, Daniel, Elijah, Paul, Peter, Luther, Huss, Latimer,

Hyde, Braynard, Peyson, Taylor, Judson, and Goforth, to mention a few.

If such unprecedented prayer power is available, why, then, do our prayers often appear to go unanswered? For one thing, there is a time to pray and a time to obey. Petition is no substitute for obedience, and you can't substitute prayer for the command of God revealed in His expressed will. In Exodus 14:15, He told Moses, "Wherefore criest thou unto me? Speak unto the children of Israel, that they go forward." Our relationship with God and obedience to His revealed will is the essential ingredient in answered prayer. The oft repeated expression, "In His name," simply means that prayer must be offered in accordance with the sum total of all He is and wills. If we are going to have real victory in prayer, then there must be total recognition of our right relationship with God.

Our Lord Jesus was ever conscious of this union and to it He gave constant testimony. "Believest thou not that I am in the Father, and the Father in me? The words that I speak unto you I speak not of myself; but the Father that dwelleth in me, he doeth the works. Believe me that I am in the Father and the Father in me: or else believe me for the very works' sake" (John 14:10–11). A little further on in the chapter He says, "At that day ye shall know that I am in my Father, and ye in me, and I in you" (v. 20). Then again, "Jesus answered and said unto him, 'If a man love me, he will keep my words: and my Father will love him, and we will come unto him and make our abode with him'" (v. 23). Doubtless this oneness is the secret of Christ's conformity to the will of His Heavenly Father. Jesus was ever on the high plane of perfect unity with God.

Christians need to recognize that by faith they are in the family of God. Through the medium of the new birth they have come into a living and vital union with God the Father and with Jesus the Son. Prayer takes on a new meaning to us when we keep this relationship in mind. There are times, no doubt, when we rise to the full height of the meaning of this glorious truth, then again we lapse into the low level of being church members with only a passing acquaintance with God.

I would not minimize church membership, but if we are to obtain real results in prayer, we must bear in mind that we are God's children, and as such, we are invited into His sacred presence for communion with Him to make known our requests. The sinner cannot be on praying ground when he spurns the only medium of approach to God—namely the Lord Jesus Christ. A backslidden Christian cannot pray successfully and he realizes it. It should be the longing of the soul of God's child to enter into the consciousness of full fellowship with God, His Son and His Spirit, and to live in unbroken communion with the triune God. As we do this, we may know with certainty that our prayers will obtain the best results. This is the secret of a successful prayer life.

Equal to our obedience to His will is the importance of our faith. Remember that two things are necessary to move the hand of God: God's willingness to bestow and my faith to believe. The Bible says, "*All* things are possible to him who [prays]," or "*All* things are possible to him that believeth." If this be true, we live in an age when there is little praying. The present condition of the church proves it. Where are the results? Plenty of praying, but few results. An age of preachers and preaching, but so little fruit. If we do not get results, we should stop and find the reason.

Man in the Garden walked by sight. But after the expulsion, he had to walk by faith; hence, the necessity of prayer as the means of communication. Prayer is a man on earth talking to God in heaven. God does nothing, but in answer to prayer. If this be true, what a tremendous responsibility rests on the believer. And remember, like people, like priest. The need of the hour is prayer—intelligent, definite, persistent prayer that will bring results, prayer which will constrain the Divine hand to come to our aid. Every child of God who has spiritual vision can see the necessity. Oh, for ministers who will set God's people to praying. Oh, for leaders to teach the saints how to pray. Oh, for servants of the Lord who will wrestle in the closet of prayer. *A revival will only come as a result of persistent prayer.* Praying preachers will have praying saints. Praying leaders will have praying followers. Praying pulpits will have praying pews. And a righteous people will, and must, pray.

The servant of God who has the spirit of prayer has power with God and man. Men who pray are men who stir up things. The man of prayer gets his sermons down instead of up, and red-hot sermons will soon warm and fill a cold church. Preaching which brings results is preaching that is born of prayer. Preaching which is saturated with prayer will hit the mark. Men of the past who have moved things for God, whose memories are fresh, and have left their mark in Christendom were all men of prayer. *Prayer will do what money, culture, learning, genius, or education cannot.* Prayer makes a heart preacher instead of a head preacher. Prayer puts the sermon on the preacher's heart. Better still, prayer puts the preacher's heart in the sermon. The preachers who are mightiest in their closets with God are the mightiest in their pulpits with men.

Prayer is the first thing, second thing, third thing necessary for the ministry. Pray, then, my brother, pray, pray, pray. Prayer makes the sermon strong, gives it unction and makes it stick. Prayer will make live sermons which will crowd the church. Preaching that kills is always prayerless preaching. Light praying will make light preaching. Truth unquickened by God's Spirit is dead, but prayer will make the Word of God quick, and powerful, and sharper than any two-edged sword.

CHAPTER 3

Our Responsibility in Prayer

Prayer has often been called "the most wonderful thing in the world." All of us have heard of the Seven Great Wonders of the World—these being the Pyramids in Egypt, the Hanging Gardens at Babylon, the Temple of Diana at Ephesus, the Statue of Jupiter at Athens, the Mausoleum at Helicarnassus, the Colossus at Rhodes, and the Pharos at Alexandria. Consider the seven great wonders of prayer, every one of which is greater than any one of the others, or of all of them combined. Those were physical, these are spiritual; those were for the glory of man, these are for the glory of God. These prayer wonders are deserving of our attention and, as experienced, of our adoring praise to our Father in heaven.

1. *The wonder that men may pray to God at all.* How marvelous that our Father should not only allow, but actually urge our petitions.

2. *The wonder that we may pray naturally and simply.* High-sounding phrases, prophetic theology, and antiquated languages are neither requested nor desired when we pray.

3. *The wonder that we may pray specifically.* Far too often our prayers are vague and general when our Lord commands us to pray specifically and pray in faith.

4. *The wonder that we may pray in all places and everywhere.*

> I will therefore that men pray everywhere, lifting up holy hands, without wrath and doubting. *1 Timothy 2:8*

5. *The wonder that we may pray all the time.* He who never slumbers or sleeps is eager to hear the voices of His children.

> Pray without ceasing. *1 Thessalonians 5:17*

6. *The wonder that we may pray about everything.* Nothing is of disinterest to Him. Nothing too large and nothing too small. If it is important to us, it is important to our Heavenly Father.

> Be careful for nothing; but in everything by prayer and supplication with thanksgiving let your requests be made known unto God. *Philippians 4:6*

7. *The wonder that we may pray boldly.* With confidence and boldness we are invited to come before His throne.

> Let us therefore come boldly unto the throne of grace, that we may obtain mercy, and find grace to help in time of need. *Hebrews 4:16*

> Thus saith the Lord, the Holy One of Israel, and his Maker, Ask me of things to come concerning my sons, and concerning the work of my hands command ye me. *Isaiah 45:11*

Sir Walter Raleigh once asked a large favor of Queen Elizabeth. The Queen lost her patience and petulantly cried, "Oh, Raleigh, when will you leave off begging?" Like a flash, Raleigh sent this answer back, *"When your*

Majesty leaves off giving." And the Queen granted Raleigh's request.

God would have like boldness from us. Only be it remembered, the God of all grace will never lose His patience with us, but will be the better pleased the bolder we are.

And why are these prayer facts prayer wonders? Because the Father to whom we pray is the Wonderful One and ever delights, in answer to prayer, to act wonderfully. Let us then match His wonderful desires toward us with our wonderful petitions toward Him until we are constrained to cry out with Isaiah of old, "O Lord, Thou art my God; I will exalt Thee, I will praise Thy name; for Thou hast done wonderful things" (Isaiah 25:1).

Prayer is being with God. Certainly you can't choose everything, but you *can* choose to be with Him. Perhaps He will take you up on the mountain with Him. Perhaps He will take you into the night with Him, or into the mist where you will not be able to see Him. Perhaps you will be with Him in pain, or in exaltation, or in tiredness, or in happiness. He just says, "Come to Me." And you say, "I will," or "I will not." You make no stipulations; that is not your part; you know that He wants you and you know what kind of wanting that is by the manger and the cross. You know that if you come to Him, He will ask you to help Him with the kingdom and will give you that work which no one else can do. You know that if you come to Him, He will ask you to help *His* friends, and that you will be allowed to bring Him into the fellowship of *your* friends. But, of course, you will also go with Him before His enemies, and the things that they say about Him will be said about you. And you will also go among the people who don't care, whom He is trying to arouse to a sense of His love. You know that He will ask you to do things that you can do only if you forget about yourself and the sort of person you thought you were; or He may ask you to face death or complete shame as He did Himself.

Prayer means that some things must go—like pride, unkindness, self-indulgence, self-importance. And all the time you will fail Him so often that by-and-by you will have no self-confidence left, only a growing confidence in Him instead . . . because He does not fail you.

"Why don't you join in our family prayers, Paul?" asked a father heatedly. This father was a pious man even though the community was more impressed by his stinginess. "I was about to pray for God's blessings on our neighbors down the road whose barn and stock were burned last night," he said. But his son was too angry to be polite: "If I had barns as well-filled as yours, I would not bother God about that. I'd answer my own prayer!"

This was a blunt answer, but not too blunt. For we assume an obligation whenever we pray. Surely we have no right to ask God to get other Christians to do what we will not do ourselves. That is why, for example, the offering belongs together with our prayer in the service! Dare I pray for blessing upon the world if my own interest and support stop outside the doors of my own church? May I pray God to send witnesses unto the uttermost parts of the earth if I consider foreign missions for "others only"?

No. As we pray, we must not forget the means of answering it. The "means" would include my offerings, and may include my going. My prayer for good government requires me to register and vote. My prayer for the sick and needy must involve visiting the neglected and ill. Real prayer is expensive. God knows when our prayers are real and deserving of an answer.

A little girl was very much worried because her brother had built some traps to catch rabbits. In spite of her tearful pleas, he refused to change his plans. Knowing this, her mother was surprised at the quiet confidence with which her daughter went to bed. When she asked about it, the little girl replied, "I prayed that God wouldn't let my little rabbits get caught in the traps. And then I went outdoors and broke the traps into a million pieces!"

Do you pray like that? If not, you aren't praying. You are "forgetting the means."

It may be well to regularly test ourselves in the area of prayer. The following questions might be called "The Christian's Aptitude Test":

Do you pray?
Do you pray daily?
Do you have family prayer?
Do you say grace at the table?
Do you pray for things you want?
Do you confess your sins daily?
Do you pray about your weakness?
Do you pray that Christ will be glorified?
Do you pray in the will of God?
Do you pray in the past, present, or future?
Do you pray for the unsaved?
Do you pray for loved ones?
Do you pray privately?
Do you pray in the morning?
Do you pray in the evening?
Do you pray over God's Word?
Do you pray about giving?

In this life we may never measure the far-reaching effects of our prayers. Prayer and giving forth God's Word are God's mighty instruments for the salvation of souls. Consider the example of the remarkable conversion of J. Hudson Taylor as related in his own words. It shows how his mother's prayers prevailed on his behalf. With gifts and talents she was not especially endowed, but she knew God, and she knew the ministry that is carried on behind the closed door. The incident reads as follows:

"Little did I know at the time what was going on in the heart of my dear mother, seventy or eighty miles away. She rose from the dinner table that afternoon with an intense yearning for the conversion of her boy, and feeling that, absent from home, and having more leisure than she could otherwise secure, a special opportunity was afforded her of pleading with God on my behalf. She went to her room and turned the key in the door, resolved not to leave that spot until her prayers were answered. Hour after hour that dear mother pled for me until at length she could pray no longer, but was constrained to praise God for that which His Spirit taught her had already been accomplished—the conversion of her only son.

"When our dear mother came home the next night, I was the first to meet her at the door and to tell her I had such glad news to give. I can almost feel that dear mother's arms around my neck as she pressed me to her bosom and said, 'I know, my boy. I have been rejoicing for a whole day in the glad tiding you have to tell me.'

"'Why?' I asked in surprise, 'Has Amelia broken her promise? She said she would tell no one.'

"My dear mother assured me that it was not from any human source that she had learned the tidings, and went on to tell the little incident mentioned above. You will agree with me that it would be strange, indeed, if I were not a believer in the power of prayer."

Oh, how great is our responsibility! How wonderful our resources! Souls are perishing on every side. Many of our relatives and loved ones are still outside the fold. We have talked to them and urged them to accept Christ, but all in vain. Year after year has gone by and they are not yet saved. Oh, that we might take upon us the burden of their souls and give God no rest until He answers and they are converted. If we truly realize that mighty instrument that God has placed in our hands, we will surely wield it until results are obtained. All else may fail, but intercessory prayer is bound to avail. God cannot deny Himself.

"I knew of a father," wrote Charles G. Finney, "who was a good man, but had erroneous views respecting the prayer of faith; and his whole family of children were grown up without one of them being converted. At length, his son sickened and seemed about to die. The father prayed, but the son grew worse, and seemed sinking into

25

the grave without hope. The father prayed til his anguish was unutterable. He went out at last and prayed (there seemed no prospect of his son surviving) so that he poured out his soul as if he would not be denied, til at length he got an assurance that his son would not only live, but would be converted; and that not only this one, but his whole family would be converted to God. He came into the house and told his family his son would not die. They were astonished at him. 'I tell you,' he said, 'He will not die. And no child of mine will ever die in his sins.' That man's children were all converted years ago."

Prayer is also the agency through which God works on behalf of His people who are in trouble.

> Peter therefore was kept in prison: but prayer was made without ceasing of the church unto God for him.
> Acts 12:5

Yes, Peter was kept in prison, such was man's power. But there follow two words that bring us immediately into a higher realm where mightier forces are at work: "but prayer." Thank God the early church knew the power of intercessory prayer. To be effective in prayer, the believer must nail down in his heart several unchangeable truths about his priorities. True and effective and powerful prayer must be from the heart. We are told to pray

1. With the heart (Lamentations 3:14);
2. With the whole heart (Jeremiah 29:13; Psalms 86:12; 119:2, 10, 34, 58, 69, 145);
3. With a true heart (Hebrews 10:22);
4. With a right heart (Job 11:13);
5. With your own heart (Psalm 4:4);
6. With a pure heart (Psalm 24:4; Matthew 5:8);
7. With a broken heart (Psalm 34:18);
8. With a fixed heart (Psalms 57:7; 108:1); and
9. With a happy heart (Ephesians 5:19).

26

We are convinced that the important link between prayer and answer is God's will. No matter who or what the desired result, we believe God will answer according to His will.

Why then should Christians pray? Will He not do as He purposes independently of what we ask? We should pray because God has bidden us. But He commands that we pray for at least three important reasons.

First, we need to pray as an act of worship, acknowledging our dependence on Him. Such prayer establishes and builds a relationship with God that grows stronger and more intimate each time we call on Him.

Second, we need to pray for the sake of our own spiritual growth and edification. Prayer does many important things for those who pray. It helps us grow in grace. It helps make us humble and aware of our dependence on God. It also brings growth because it leads to the exercise of our faith. Indeed, there is no better way to test your faith. Many people, like a little girl I know, pray with one eye open, wondering whether God will answer, but that is not exercising faith. Prayer also teaches us the value of blessings. What we work for we appreciate. If God makes blessings dependent on our asking, we see the value of these blessings.

The third reason why we should pray is that God wants us to request His gifts. There are many who say that because God is good and wise, prayer is not necessary. This is wrong, for prayer is not an act of begging from God something He did not intend for us to have. Prayer is giving God an opportunity to do what He wants to do without encountering unreadiness and faithlessness in us.

There are things He cannot do until we allow Him to do them in and through us. There are things He cannot say until we are ready to listen or to permit Him to say through us. There are things He cannot give until we allow Him to give them to us or through us. We ought to think of prayer in terms of the story of a king whose son was going away from his father's palace to live in a palace of his own. As he was leaving, he was told that he should return once a year to receive all he needed for the coming twelve months. Unable to bear the long separation, however, the king first advised his son that he should come once a month, then once a week, and finally every day to let his needs be known and to receive the desires of his heart.

God is perfectly capable of making provision for our every need with one grand and final gesture. But with a desire for fellowship and to help man see his true dependence on Him, He has made His bounty dependent on our daily prayer of faith.

The very fact that men may pray is something indeed. In helplessness or hopelessness to be able to reach out and touch infinite resources surely is one of life's greatest benedictions. Standing amid what seem to be impossible situations—such as moral degeneracy, political corruption, social vices, individual hatreds—being able to pray, believing that something can be done, is heartening. It spurs the disciple on and on so that he feels confident that some good may come of a bad situation.

When we read, "Ask what ye will and it shall be done unto you" and "All things are possible to him that believeth," we wonder why we cannot rid the world of war, society of sin, men of their failures. Then earth, it seems, would become our footstool and heaven our throne. We seem to see the green light of prayer flashing before us that will open the doors to an everlasting life of victory, then when we fail to see the walls come tumbling down and society freed from the curses of sin, we are thrown into confusion. We complain that prayer is a mockery, that God does not make good His promises, and of all people, the man of prayer is most miserable.

Stop! Before you see the green light you should see the red light.

Before you "go," you might "tarry."
Before you "speak," you might "think."
Before you "receive," you might "sow."
Before you "acquire," you might "give."
Before you "pray," you might "listen."

Our Lord was, of course, the ultimate example of intercessory prayer.

> But I have prayed for thee, that thy faith fail not: and when thou art converted, strengthen thy brethren. And he said unto him, Lord, I am ready to go with thee, both into prison, and to death. And he said, I tell thee, Peter, the cock shall not crow this day, before that thou shalt thrice deny that thou knowest me. *Luke 22:32–34*

As His disciples, we too are exhorted to pray. Here are but a few of the things that are the object of the believer's prayer.

1. All in authority (1 Timothy 2:2);
2. Ministers (2 Corinthians 1:11; Philippians 1:19);
3. The community of God's people (Psalm 122:6; Isaiah 62:6–7);
4. All saints (Ephesians 6:18);
5. Masters (Genesis 24:12–14);
6. Servants (Luke 7:2–3);
7. Children (Genesis 17:18; Matthew 15:22);
8. Fellow countrymen (Romans 10:1);
9. The sick (James 5:14);
10. Persecutors (Matthew 5:44);
11. Those who envy (Numbers 12:1–13);
12. Those who forsake (2 Timothy 4:16); and
13. Those who murmur against God (Numbers 11:1–2; 14:2, 19).

Real prayer takes time and demands the best of our efforts and priorities. The late Dr. John Henry Jowett said that he was once in a most pitiable perplexity and consulted Dr. Berry of Wolverhampton. "What would you do if you were in my place?" he asked.

"I don't know, Jowett. I am not there, and you are not there yet. When do you have to act?"

"On Friday," Dr. Jowett replied.

"Then you will find' your way perfectly clear on Friday. The Lord will not fail you," answered Berry. And sure enough, on Friday, all was plain.

One of the greatest and wisest of all Queen Victoria's diplomats has left it on record that it became an inveterate habit of his mind never to allow any opinion on any subject to crystallize until it became necessary to arrive at a practical decision.

Give God time, and even when the knife flashes in the air, the ram will be seen caught in the thicket.

Give God time, and even when Pharaoh's host is on Israel's heels, a path through the waters will be suddenly open.

Give God time, and when the bed of the brook is dry, Elijah shall hear the guiding voice.

James, the brother of our Lord and the author of the epistle bearing his name, was nicknamed "Camel Knees" by the early church. When they came to bury him, it was like coffining the knees of a camel rather than the knees of a man—they were so hard, so stiff, so worn from prayer, it is said. When "Praying Hyde" died, they found thick calluses on his knees as well. *How are your knees?*

A hundred volumes could not contain the blessings of God that await those who pray.

> *Strength:* "Seek the Lord, and his strength: seek his face evermore" *(Psalm 105:4).*
>
> *Whatsoever:* "Verily, verily, I say unto you, Whatsoever ye shall ask the Father in my name, he will give it you. Hitherto have ye asked nothing in my name: ask, and ye shall receive, that your joy may be full" *(John 16:23–24).*

Divine Nearness: "The Lord is nigh unto all them that call upon him, to all that call upon him in truth" *(Psalm 145:18).*

Wisdom: "If any of you lack wisdom, let him ask of God, that giveth to all men liberally, and upbraideth not; and it shall be given him. But let him ask in faith, nothing wavering. For he that wavereth is like a wave of the sea driven with the wind and tossed. For let not that man think that he shall receive any thing of the Lord" *(James 1:5–7).*

Help for Infirmity: "Likewise the Spirit also helpeth our infirmities: for we know not what we should pray for as we ought: but the Spirit itself maketh intercession for us with groanings which cannot be uttered" *(Romans 8:26).*

Lifting Up: "Draw nigh to God, and he will draw nigh to you. Cleanse your hands, ye sinners; and purify your hearts, ye double-minded. . . . Humble yourselves in the sight of the Lord, and he shall lift you up" *(James 4:8, 10).*

Mercy and Grace: "Let us therefore come boldly unto the throne of grace, that we may obtain mercy, and find grace to help in time of need" *(Hebrews 4:16).*

Forgiveness: "If we confess our sins, he is faithful and just to forgive us our sins, and to cleanse us from all unrighteousness" *(1 John 1:9).*

Deliverance from Trouble: "The righteous cry, and the Lord heareth, and delivereth them out of all their troubles" *(Psalm 34:17).*

Deliverance from Enemies: "When I cry unto thee, then shall mine enemies turn back: this I know; for God is for me" *(Psalm 56:9).*

Gift of the Holy Spirit: "If ye then, being evil, know how to give good gifts unto your children: how much more shall your heavenly Father give the Holy Spirit to them that ask him?" *(Luke 11:13).*

Knowledge: "Yea, if thou criest after knowledge, and liftest up thy voice for understanding; . . . Then shalt thou understand the fear of the Lord, and find the knowledge of God" *(Proverbs 2:3, 5).*

Honor: "He shall call upon me, and I will answer him: I will be with him in trouble; I will deliver him, and honour him" *(Psalm 91:15).*

But our Lord clearly teaches that we are to pray for others as well. John Ballie has said it well:

> *Especially do I commend to Thy holy keeping, Lord:*
>   *All who tonight are far from home and friends;*
>   *All who tonight must lie down hungry or cold;*
>   *All who suffer pain;*
>   *All who are kept awake by anxiety or suspense;*
>   *All who are facing danger;*
>   *All who must toil or keep watch while others sleep.*
>
> *Give to them all, I pray, such a sense of Thy presence with them as may turn their loneliness into comfort and their trouble into peace.*

In prayer it is better to have a heart without words than to have words without a heart.

Prayer must mean something to us if it is to mean anything to God.

Prayer is the pitcher that fetcheth water from the brook wherewith to water the herbs; break the pitcher, and it will fetch no water, and for want of water the garden will wither.

You can do more than pray after you have prayed, but you cannot do more than pray until you have prayed.

Prayer is not overcoming God's reluctance; it is laying hold of His highest willingness.

A preacher began his sermon by saying, "Brethren and sisters, here you are coming to pray for rain. I'd like to ask you just one question—where are your umbrellas?"

If you won't talk to God on a clear day, there isn't much use in yelling at Him in a storm.

A little motive cannot live in a big prayer.

CHAPTER 4

Praying the Bible Way

Our intent in this book, as with *The Power of Positive Praying,* is to help you to learn not only the power and privilege of prayer, but the practical aspects of "how to pray."

In every sense of the word, the Bible is a book of prayer. Each verse was given with the breath of God who moved on holy men of old to record His work. If prayer is communion with God, and if it is the medium of His Word through which He speaks, it quite naturally follows that it is through that same medium that we best speak to Him. Nothing may bring us more into the divine presence than praying God's words back to Him. In taking the time to pray over, through, and with the Word of God, the believer finds himself more at union with the Father than through any other spiritual exercise. Better than praying, better than reading the Word—literally praying the Word is truly "praying the Bible way."

"Praying the Word" begins in getting physically alone with God in the secret closet of prayer. It is in the quietest seclusion that we find the Master awaits His own. A comfortable place in which to kneel, a small light in a darkened room, and a translation of the Bible with which you are comfortable are all that is required. From Genesis to Revelation, you need not read far until the Spirit impresses on your heart an affinity to a particular verse or passage. Whatever arrests the attention of the soul is the touch of the Spirit's finger on your immediate need. When it grips you, stop and re-read. Read it three times in your heart, and three times aloud. Then, with eyes closed, pray those verses to the Father, inserting your own personality and need therein.

The Master set the classic example of secret prayer. Early in His ministry He found it necessary to withdraw to the desert and pray:

> But so much the more went there a fame abroad of him: and great multitudes came together to hear, and to be healed by him of their infirmities. And he withdrew himself into the wilderness, and prayed. *Luke 5:15–16*

Earlier that day He had prayed alone:

> And in the morning, rising up a great while before day, he went out, and departed into a solitary place, and there prayed. *Mark 1:35*

Long prayers, like long sermons, often only indicate a lack of preparation. Charles Haddon Spurgeon has well said,

> Brethren, in all things has our Lord Jesus given us the best example—also in regard to praying. When with His disciples, His prayers were of medium length. In the midst of a large crowd, as at Lazarus' grave and the feeding of the five thousand, His prayer was short. When He was alone with His Father, in the Garden or on the Mount—then He prayed all night. So ought ye also to do, dear brethren. Among God's children, make your prayer of medium length as Jesus did when He was about to be crucified, when in a crowd or with the sick or dying or the unfortunate, short. When you

are alone with your Father in your secret closet, pray as long as you please.

One of the great delights of prayer is that we may pray anywhere. Abraham's servant prayed by his camel, Isaac in the field, Jacob by a brook, and Jeremiah in a dungeon. David prayed at a cave and Peter on a housetop. Jonah prayed in a fish and Hezekiah prayed before a wall. The similarity between them all—they prayed in the secret place.

Prayer is getting into touch with God. Jesus says that we should do it when we enter our closet and shut the door. It means shutting out the world. I have an idea that Jesus may not have been thinking so much here of a physical closet and a physical door; to be physically alone helps, but I rather think Jesus means here to get alone with God. We are to shut out the world with its clamor and noise, and we can do that on the busy street, on the railroad train, right in the midst of the hustle and bustle of life. Sometimes we must do it there if at all. But every effort *should* be made to establish a physical prayer altar in a secret place.

A Christian woman told me once about being greatly disturbed in mind and heart. She had no time to herself, no opportunity to shut a physical door and be alone with God. She worked long hours every day with people all around her. She sought God in prayer, prayed without ceasing as she worked, until perfect peace came to her. It might have been easier had she been differently situated. But she *shut out* the world right *in the midst* of the world.

We need to shut out the world, but that is not the end of it. We shut out the world in order to be shut in with God. Prayer is making connection. It is fellowship with God. Jesus says; "Pray to thy Father who is in secret." I am impressed with that saying: "Thy Father who is in secret." God is not a public figure. He is a God who hides Himself as well as a God who reveals Himself. He never pushes

Himself on people. He is too much of a gentleman for that. Sometimes we break in where we are not wanted. He never does—He delights to reveal Himself to those who seek Him.

There is really no such thing as public prayer. There is such a thing as prayer in public places. In form, a congregation may approach and worship God, but the essence of prayer is inner relationship with the God who is in secret. It is an unseen transaction between the soul of man and the invisible God. It is a transaction that no eye of man can see.

The place of prayer may well include not only a Bible and a light, but a favorite hymnbook. What a joy to sing alone with our Lord, "Open My Eyes That I May See," "Sweet Hour of Prayer," or "Take Time to Be Holy!" With music, with His presence, and with His Word the quiet place becomes the best place.

Souls often get lonely in a crowd and starve amid temples, worshipers, and ordinances. God would have us alone with Him sometimes, but remember that coming to church is not coming to Christ. "Enter into thy closet and shut the door." Shut out nonsense, business, care, and pleasure. Shut out flatteries. Shut out friends and foes. Shut out this world and open the window that looks out upon the next.

Give the mind rest. Give the ear quiet. Give the tongue silence. Give the heart meditation. Give the soul communion with God. Look up! There are blessings waiting for you. Listen! God speaks in His still, small voice. Ask! God waits to hear. See that no shade of sin hides from your sight the heavenly Father's face.

Settle the question of peace, pardon, and duty in secret before the Lord; then bring everything that concerns your heart and life, for time and for eternity, and lay it before the mercy-seat. "In every thing by prayer and supplication with thanksgiving let your requests be made known unto God. And the peace of God, which passeth all understanding, shall keep your hearts and minds through Christ Jesus" (Philippians 4:6–7).

> There is a place where thou canst touch the eyes
>   Of blinded men to instant perfect sight;
> There is a place where thou canst say "Arise!"
>   To dying captives bound in chains of night;
> There is a place where thou canst reach the store
>   Of hoarded gold and free it for the Lord;
> There is a place here or on a distant shore
>   Where thou canst send the worker and the Word.
> There is a place where Heaven's resistless power
>   Responsive moves to this insistent plea;
> There is a place, a silent holy hour
>   Where God Himself descends and works for thee
> Where is that secret place—dost thou ask where?
>   Oh, soul, it is the secret place of prayer.

Twice in 2 Corinthians Paul speaks beautifully to the openness of the whole man before God.

> For we are not, like so many (as hucksters, tavern keepers, making a trade of) peddling God's Word— short-measuring and adulterating the divine message; but as [men] of sincerity and the purest motive, commissioned and sent by God, we speak [His message] in Christ, the Messiah, in the [very] sight and presence of God. *2 Corinthians 2:17 Amplified*

> Have you been supposing [all this time] that we have been defending ourselves and apologizing to you? [It is] in the sight and the [very] presence of God [and as one] in Christ, the Messiah, that we have been speaking, dearly beloved, and all in order to build you up [spiritually]. *2 Corinthians 12:19 Amplified*

Fellowship with God in the communion of prayer opens our hearts to Him and His Word and is most naturally and practically experienced as we hear His Word, put ourselves into His Word, and *pray His Word back to Him*. Consider, for example, the beautiful benediction of Paul in Ephesians 3:16–19:

May He grant you out of the rich treasury of His glory to be strengthened and reinforced with mighty power in the inner man by the (Holy) Spirit [Himself]—indwelling your innermost being and personality.

May Christ through your faith [actually] dwell—settle down, abide, make His permanent home—in your hearts! May you be rooted deep in love and founded securely on love, that you may have the power and be strong to apprehend and grasp with all the saints (God's devoted people, the experience of that love) what is the breadth and length and height and depth [of it]; [That you may really come] to know—practically, which far surpasses mere knowledge (without experience); that you may be filled (through all your being) unto all the fullness of God—[that is] may have the richest measure of the divine Presence, and become a body wholly filled and flooded with God Himself! (Amplified)

Memorizing, praying over, assimilating, and paraphrasing this passage, one might pray in this manner:

Father, I acknowledge that it is of the riches of your grace and glory that I have my strength. Reinforce me, empower me to the very depth of my personality with Thyself. Oh God, grow down deep into the depths of my soul. Let me know the height, breadth, and depth of your person. I open myself to Thee that Thou mayest fill my being with the fullest measure of the presence of Thy divine self.

George Mueller, in his autobiography Life and Trust, stated, "I have read the Bible through from Genesis to Revelation ninety times. I do not read and pray for a sermon. I do not pray for a Bible lesson. I read and pray for spiritual food for my soul." The Word of God is the point at which God meets man and fellowships with him. All things are possible for them that believe. And how are we to believe? "So then faith cometh by hearing, and hearing by the word of God" (Romans 10:17).

In the Word we *see* Him. In the Word we *know* Him. He waits to open the windows of heaven for those who pray according to His will, and that will may only be known *through His Word.* Through His Word He speaks to us, and through His Word we may naturally speak to Him. The time spent in learning to "pray the Word of God" may be the richest experiences of the prayer life.

May our heavenly Father move upon His own, stirring our hearts to learn to pray the Bible way.

CHAPTER 5

Special Prayers

Using the Word of God in prayer, making it our own, putting ourselves in its truths, and praying His words back to the Father in the quietness of the secret place deeply enriches the prayer life of the believer. Four special kinds of prayer using the Scripture may be suggested to those who would learn to pray the Bible way.

1. *The Prayer of Daily Commitment.* As followers of the Lamb, the believer is subject daily to the world, the flesh, and the Devil. Each morning the totality of human personhood must be committed under the covering of Christ, the only place that brings refuge from this trinity of enemies to the soul.

One of the lovely promises of Exodus states:

> And the blood shall be to you for a token upon the houses where ye are: and when I see the blood, I will pass over you, and the plague shall not be upon you to destroy you, when I smite the land of Egypt. *Exodus 12:13*

The word "token" means an evident sign of authority. It is the place of safety and security. The promise of God is that beneath the authority of the blood, there is shelter from without. A lovely prayer at the dawning of each new day might go as follows:

> I commit my mind to the shelter of the blood of Christ, that it shall not wander astray from God's will. . . . I commit my thoughts to the efficacy of the blood of Christ, that they may be pure and edifying; I commit my will . . . that it shall be His continually; I commit my desires . . . that they shall be set upon no vain thing; . . . my motives, that my eye might be single for His glory; . . . my affections, that they might be set upon things above; my imaginations . . . that I might be practical, and spiritually minded; . . . my personality, that it might witness for Him; I commit my body; . . . my entire being, to the shelter and efficacy of the blood of Christ that nothing shall come to me from the enemy that has not been filtered through Thy perfect will.
>
> He who once gave His blood for us, will every moment, impart its efficacy. Trust Him above all, to work out in you, unceasingly, the full merits of His blood, so that your whole life may be an uninterrupted abiding in the sanctuary of God's presence. *Hebrews 10: 19–22; Revelation 7:9–14 Paraphrased*

Our Lord is faithful to His Word. When in faith we commit ourselves to the security He promises beneath His keeping power, we may be confidently assured that the place of victory and safety is secured. No more should the believer walk into the day without this covering than walk amid nuclear warfare without adequate armor.

2. The Prayer of Committal. At any given time we are confronted with burdened hearts over friends and loved ones or situations that trouble us. The songwriter has appropriately said, "Oh, what peace we often forfeit, oh, what needless pain we bear, all because we do not carry everything to God in prayer." Most of us know what the writer intended. All of us have had the experience of taking the problems of our lives and those of our loved ones to the Father in prayer. But it is the *leaving them there* that is difficult. In the prayer of committal we totally deposit in the able charge of a loving heavenly Father every need of every situation and every person about which we are burdened. Our Lord gave us the example when on the cross He prayed, "Father, into thy hands I commend [commit] my spirit" (Luke 23:46). Peter followed in his Lord's footsteps when he said,

> Wherefore let them that suffer according to the will of God commit the keeping of their souls to him in well-doing, as unto a faithful Creator. *1 Peter 4:19*

Paul reminds us that God has totally deposited in the charge of His children the dissemination of the gospel.

> To wit, that God was in Christ, reconciling the world unto himself, not imputing their trespasses unto them; and hath committed unto us the word of reconciliation. *2 Corinthians 5:19*

The writer of Proverbs reminds us,

> Commit thy works unto the Lord, and thy thoughts shall be established. *Proverbs 16:3*

When John, in his first epistle, charged that "whosoever is born of God doth not commit sin (3:9), he was saying that we never wholly give a committal back over to a life of sin. Biblical committal does not mean to toy with something from time to time; rather, to totally give it up and over to another. There are burdens too hard to bear, loved ones impossible to help, problems too difficult to solve. In such cases, the prayer of committal is to be used. In this prayer one might speak in this manner: "Father, this person, this problem is yours. It is beyond me, but not beyond Thee. I commit it to you with all its ramifications, leaving it totally in the charge of your capable hands."

3. *The Prayer of Blessing.*

And he led them out as far as to Bethany, and he lifted up his hands, and blessed them. *Luke 24:50*

Bless them which persecute you: bless, and curse not. *Romans 12:14*

The biblical concept of blessing others has nearly been lost to our generation. Little enough heart and verbal blessing is done to those we love. Virtually none is bestowed on those we dislike, although Christ taught us to bless our enemies, those who persecute and are cruel to us. Frankly, a verbal blessing on someone who has just cussed us out will likely only add fuel to the fire. But a blessing from the heart in response to antagonism can be the gentle response—the other cheek that turns away wrath. Arguments between husbands and wives can turn to sweetness when repeated prayers of "I bless you in the name of Jesus" come from the heart of the injured mate. Let children learn to bless their parents; employees, their employers; married persons, their spouses, and sweetness will abound.

The first occasion of blessing of someone you resent may be very difficult, but the second or third time will come more easily. Think of the Master at Calvary. Review the events of that final Friday and hear Him, forsaken of all men, say at the last, "Father, forgive them; for they know not what they do" (Luke 23:34).

4. *The Seven Prayers of Praise.* In Psalm 119:164 David writes, "Seven times a day do I praise thee because of thy righteous judgments." The number seven is a biblical symbol for completion. As "praise becometh the Lord," complete and becoming praise in the mind of the psalmist may well have been based on the seven redemptive names of Jehovah.

> *Jehovah—jireh:* "The Lord will provide"
> *Jehovah—rapha:* "The Lord that healeth"
> *Jehovah—nissi:* "The Lord, our banner" (victory is wholly due to divine help)

Jehovah—shalom: "The Lord, our peace"
Jehovah—ra-ah: "The Lord, my shepherd"
Jehovah—tsidkenu: "The Lord, our righteousness"
Jehovah—shammah: "The Lord is there"

These names or titles for Jehovah are descriptive of His work in relation to men blessing Him at seven different times through the day by invoking His name to bring a marvelous sense of the divine presence. Memorize these titles and pray the Bible way, blessing the Lord with them.

CHAPTER 6

When It Seems God Doesn't Answer

And as Jesus passed by, he saw a man which was blind from his birth. And his disciples asked him, saying, Master, who did sin, this man or his parents, that he was born blind? Jesus answered, Neither hath this man sinned, nor his parents: but that the works of God should be made manifest in him. I must work the works of him that sent me, while it is day: the night cometh, when no man can work. As long as I am in the world, I am the light of the world. *John 9:1–5*

As Jesus and His disciples were passing by, His followers were captivated by the sight of a blind man waiting by the wayside begging. Several questions raced through their minds. Why was he blind? What was behind this illness? Could there be any sense to it? What had he done wrong? Surely he must have been a wicked man to experience the judgment of God in such a devastating way.

But the Bible says the man did not become blind; he was born that way. He had never seen a sunrise. He had never seen the lush, green grass, the beautiful blue hues of a sky put into the heavens by a loving Father. He lived in a closed world separated from family and friends, rejected by society, apparently cursed by God. But why? Why him? Why this?

The attitude of the disciples ran parallel to the current thought of the day that sin and suffering were soul brothers. However, the Book of Job soundly contradicts this idea. Not all suffering is caused by sin.

God said that Job was "perfect and upright." He was a man who continually feared God and fled from evil. He was a man whose number one priority was his family. Daily and constantly he interceded in their behalf, providing a "spiritual cover" for his wife and children. Together God and Job had "built a hedge" about himself, his family, and all his possessions.

The Devil said, "Job serves God only because of this hedge of protection." In His permissive will, God permitted Satan to harass Job's family and Job himself. Yet Job was faithful. God honored his faithfulness and gave living proof to the fact that suffering is not always related to sin, though it sometimes is.

From the passage in John 9 we discover that God's purpose in permitting the suffering of the blind man was that His glory may be manifested. The testimony of Christians amid trial and tribulation has always spoken to the glory of God and the sufficiency of His grace. While we try to figure everything out, God is saying, "Lean not unto thine own understanding. In all thy ways acknowledge him, and he shall direct thy paths" (Proverbs 3:5–6). The acknowledgment of God amid suffering permits the manifestation of God, which gives glory to God. Tragedy moves swiftly into triumph when God is glorified.

At the point of man's extremity there is the beautiful awareness of God's opportunity to gain the glory that is justly due a holy and righteous God. Many blessings are missed because God's people fail to understand sorrow and suffering when prayer to remove them is unanswered.

1. God's Perspective Is Different from Man's.

> For my thoughts are not your thoughts, neither are
> your ways my ways, saith the Lord. For as the heavens
> are higher than the earth, so are my ways higher than
> your ways, and my thoughts than your thoughts. *Isaiah
> 55:8–9*

God's perspective is an eternal perspective. He is the
Alpha and Omega. He sees the beginning and the ending.
He knows each chapter of our lives and knows the fullness
of our lives.

Our perspective is a temporal, earthly one. God sees
things not only as they are, but as they *were* and as they
will be. Every infinitesimal part of our life is viewed
panoramically as part of the whole, moment by moment,
in minute detail before a majestic God from on high. God
eclipses human reasoning, eliminating friction and frag-
mentation of truth. The affirmation of God, who knows
and understands the whole of life, frees us to understand,
as best we can, the godly wisdom of sorrow and suffering.

I heard from a friend the story of a prosperous
businessman who had never been ill but, suddenly
confined in a hospital bed, was trying to deal with the
problem of suffering. My friend was led on one occasion to
read several pages of Scripture. Before leaving the patient's
room, he bowed his head in prayer and said something like
this:

> Lord, we are thankful for the commitment of our
> friend. He doesn't understand why he is suffering as he
> is, nor why You appear not to answer his prayer. Help
> him to realize that You are the Divine Composer of
> life's musical score. Time is very important in the
> composition of music. The composer fills the score
> with 32nd notes and 16th notes and 8th notes, and
> then he chooses to insert a rest. Sometimes it is a
> quarter rest, sometimes a half rest. But the composer
> knows that the rests in the music are very important.
> They give balance to the composition. So, dear Lord,
> today we thank You for inserting a rest in the midst of
> the hectic pace of my dear friend.

Having finished the prayer, the businessman looked up through tears and said, "Thank you for helping to see that God is busy making the music of my life sweeter."

Not now, but in the coming years,
It may be in the better land,
We'll read the meaning of our tears,
And there, sometime, we'll understand.

We'll catch the broken thread again,
And finish what we here began,
Heav'n will the mysteries explain,
And then, ah, then, we'll understand.

Why, what we long for most of all,
Eludes so oft our eager grasp,
Why, dreams are crushed and castles fall,
Sometime, someday, we'll understand.

God holds the key, He knows the way,
He guides us with unerring hand.
Someday through tearless eyes we'll see,
And there, up there, we'll understand.
—Maxwell N. Cornelius

2. *God's Plan Is on a Different Level Than Man's.* Isaiah wrote, "As the mountains are high above the earth, even so are God's ways higher than your ways." God's strategy is based on supernatural knowledge. His working plan supersedes the highest level that man could ever hope to obtain.

God's wisdom permits Him to intercede in our lives, protecting us from danger. As a loving mother protects her child from a hotplate, God protects us from devastating dangers of which we are oblivious.

Let us recall the story in Numbers 21 of the children of Israel making their way to the Promised Land. On one occasion in the heated desert, they were mercilessly attacked by fiery serpents. Turning right and left, the Israelites were faced only with the option of how soon death would come.

Moses pleaded desperately with God, "Lord, we are not going to survive, the fiery serpents are playing havoc with our people, We are going to die, What shall we do?"

God's instructions to Moses seemed deplorable. "Make a serpent of brass and place it on a pole, and it shall come to pass that whoever will look will live." Surely questions raced through Moses' mind as he obeyed the command of the Lord. He placed a brass serpent on a pole and, according to the promise, healing came to the dying victims. God's plan was not to destroy the serpent, but to provide a cure. God's ways are always effective though sometimes they seem strange to us. But amid chaos, God brings forth calm. Amid tragedy, God brings forth triumph.

Years ago I read the story about a father and his son. The father, a wonderful Christian farmer, did not have the opportunity for higher learning, but wanted to see to it that his son got the best. Upon the son's returning from his freshman year at college, father and son were standing under a tree on the farm, and the father began to interrogate his son about his experiences at the university.

The young man said, "Dad, I enjoyed my first year in school, but you know, I studied biology and philosophy and botany and I have learned some things that have upset me."

The father was curious to know what was troubling his son. The young man replied, "Dad, I have discovered that God made the world wrong. For example, look at this strong oak tree under which we stand. God placed a small acorn on it. And look to our right at that big pumpkin. God placed it on a fragile vine! I would have put the big pumpkin on the sturdy oak."

About that time, the wind blew and an acorn fell off the tree and hit the college student on the head. The boy mopped his brow, looked at his father, and said, "Gee, Dad, thank God it wasn't a pumpkin!"

God's plan is always best, His ways always perfect. We

need desperately to learn to trust Him when an answer does not come. The psalmist said, "Commit thy way unto the Lord; trust also in him; and he shall bring it to pass" (Psalm 37:5).

The independent heart that says, "I can make it alone; I did it my way; I don't need anyone," will only self-destruct. History reminds us that the foolish man is the man left alone to his own devices. Apart from God we are nothing. God accepts man as he is and moves in his life to lead him where he should be. Surely the early Christian prayed that God would remove wicked Saul who became Paul, a servant of the Lord. God's difference makes the difference! His ways are wise, His strategy sound, and His techniques trustworthy.

3. *God's Program Is Timeless.* God's agenda is not limited by His relationship to time. In 2 Peter 3:8 we recall that a thousand years are to God as one day. We say that time is of the utmost importance, but God is never in a hurry. He measures time by eternity. To God, the essence of time is life, and it is intended to be full and abundant. We need to realize that with God time has no barriers. Often the fullness of life is discovered only as we wait on the Lord. The psalmist says,

> "My soul, wait thou only upon God; for my expectation is from him" *(Psalm 62:5)*.

> "Our soul waiteth for the Lord: he is our help and our shield" *(33:20)*.

> "My times are in thy hand" *(31:15)*.

God's seeming unanswering of prayer may, in fact, be a very positive answer: *Wait.*

Throughout the New Testament we see Jesus always composed. Everything that He did was done deliberately. There was order; there was clarity; there was an unruffled destiny in every step He took. Jesus would not be rushed. He would never be hurried. At the wedding in Cana, when the host ran out of wine, Jesus' mother feverishly urged Him to do something. He told her, "Mine hour is not yet come" (John 2:4). God's timing is perfect. If we will discover the blessing of waiting upon the Lord, we shall discover renewed strength as well. And we shall learn something about answered prayer. Ours is but to learn to "run with patience the race that is set before us" (Hebrews 12:1).

The intimacy of time alone with God when we have been set aside in sickness, in sorrow, or in suffering is more precious than words can describe and can teach us the joy of waiting for the revelation of His purposes.

Growth comes through struggle. Suffering strengthens us. When the gears of life are moved to neutral or reverse, the presence of God becomes more real and precious than ever before. The hour of trial removes the dross, supplants the superficial, and produces the fiber that strengthens our faith. Suffering and sorrow in life patiently endured will produce a new sense of godly priorities.

Fearful questions amid dark shadows produce faltering steps. Our is rather to trust completely in the perfect work of God who is the same "yesterday, today, and forever." I learned as a little child that shadows did not hurt me. I learned as well that the shadows in life were only present because there was a greater light. May we as God's children look toward the greater light in Jesus Christ and trust Him in the midnight hour as well as at daybreak. In time of personal discouragement, I am reminded of the words of a friend, "Don't worry, the sun will rise again."

Someone has said it all much better than I could ever say in the words of the old hymn,

> *God works in most mysterious ways,*
> *His wonders to perform.*
> *He plants his footprints on the sea,*
> *And rides upon the storm.*

Deep in unfathomable mines,
Of never dying skill,
He treasures up His bright design,
And works His sovereign will.

Ye trembling saints, fresh courage take,
The cloud you so much dread,
Is filled with mercy, and will break
With blessings on your head.

Judge not the Lord with feeble sense,
But trust Him for His grace,
Behind the mask of providence,
God wears a smiling face.

His purposes will ripen fast,
Unfolding every hour,
The bud may have a bitter taste,
But sweet will be the flower.

Blind unbelief is sure to err,
And scan His work in vain,
God is His own interpreter,
And He will make it plain.
                    —William Cowper

CHAPTER 7

Learning to Wait for Answers

When I was young, I told God what to do,
    And called it prayer.
Even the questions that I asked of you
    I let Him share.

There were so many things He might not see—
    That was my fear;
I told Him ways of secret ecstasy;
    He would not hear.

Now that I'm old, I have been taught to see
    The unspoilt sweetness that is yesterday.
Without a future, man at last is free.
    With nought to ask for, I have learnt to pray.

A man with a great burden on his soul was praying earnestly for help and strength. He pleaded with deep fervency and tried to listen for an answer, but nothing happened. Finally, after almost an hour, he discovered that an old religious song was singing itself in the back of his mind. It was one he had heard many times in his youth, but which he had not sung or heard for years. In fact, only one phrase of the song was clear: "Near to the heart of God." He could hear the tune, but he could hear none of the words, except those six.

With a sense of great relief the man seized those words, claimed them as his answer, and prayed: "O God, that must have been thy voice speaking to me. At least, I am going to believe it to be true. I am going to accept those words as my answer and trust them." Within a few minutes his spirit was at rest, and his soul was calm under the terrific pressure it was bearing.

God speaks in so many ways. The mood of quiet that comes without any explanation that steals over us; the calm feeling of confidence that sometimes overtakes us; the sudden leaping to life of our determination to achieve, to master temptation, to improve—all these things are evidence of the fact that we are dealing with God and not merely some psychological phenomenon.

Prayer is like a game. There are rules to follow. If you would really find the secrets of prayer, you must know the rules. You don't play a game without rules; you don't bake a cake without a recipe; you don't build a house without blueprints; you don't pray successfully without following the fundamentals in prayer.

Prayer is an experience with God, based on a moral order, not an intellectual order. Prayer is based on deeds, not words. Prayer is based on fellowship, not merely conversation. Let us look at the negative side for a moment to see why we do not realize more out of our prayer life.

"Blessed are the pure in heart: for they shall see God." Impurity of life (moral order) blinds the vision of God.

"If I regard iniquity in my heart [moral order], the Lord will not hear." Sin closes the door.

"A double-minded man, unstable in all his ways, let not that man think he will receive anything from the Lord." God does not place answers in the hands of irresponsible people.

"You have made the house of prayer a den of thieves. Get out!" He said.

"If my words abide in you, ask what you will, it will be granted."

If we surrender our lives and hearts to Him and will walk in His ways, we will experience His presence, His power, and His answers. We will have discovered the way to answered prayer. It may not be what we want, but it will be what is best for us in life and in fellowship with both God and man. God is a prayer-answering God. It is the attitude we have toward Him that makes the difference.

A lady stepped from the curb into the street and held up her hand to stop a bus. It looked as if she had the fare in her uplifted hand. It seemed she had met all conditions for riding on this bus. Yet, although it slowed down, the bus did not stop.

Vexed and disappointed, the woman looked with indignant inquiry at the driver who had surely seen her. But in a moment a look of relief and resignation came over her face, for she realized that, *in denying her request to ride, the driver was really helping her get where she wanted to go.* His bus was going to the bus garage.

How often the child of God, feeling he has met every condition of answered prayer, reads the sign, TAKE THE NEXT CAR. Sometimes God is arranging for us the speediest possible answer, when at the time, our prayer is answered "no."

> He was a Christian and he prayed. He asked for strength to do greater things, but he was given infirmity that he might do better things.
>
> He asked for riches that he might be happy; he was given poverty that he might be wise.
>
> He asked for power that he might have the praise of men; he was given weakness that he might feel the need of God.
>
> He had received nothing that he asked for; but *all that he had hoped for.* His prayer seems unanswered, but he is most blessed.

All answers to prayer may be divided into three classes. If I want a sum of money and ask God for it, He may answer me in one of three ways: (1) He may give me the money in hand; (2) He may give me ability to earn it; or (3) He may give me grace to do without it.

It is a very serious thing to pray. The real seriousness comes not in the possibility that our prayer may not be answered; the appallingly serious thing is that *it may be answered.* A real answer to prayer will usually let us in for more than we asked for. A man prays for strength, for instance, without much thought of the matter, as though strength could be wrapped up in a package like a pound of sugar and handed to one. Strength must be grown; it comes from struggle against obstacles. *The only way in which a prayer for strength can be answered is by putting a man into a place where he will have to struggle.* We ought to be careful before we ask for strength. God might overhear us and answer us. So it is with frequent prayer that we have the spirit of Jesus. Many people make that prayer thoughtlessly without realizing that if they really had the spirit of Jesus, it would knock them and their whole world upside down.

Why did Satan have the victory? Frank D. Bundy, Central American Mission missionary in Guatemala, turned the matter over in his mind. The mission property at Panajachel needed enlargement. An adjoining lot was for sale by an Indian woman, and measurements were being taken with the woman present. All was ready for completing the purchase. The dream of many months seemed about to come true, and hearts were glad at this answer to prayer.

Suddenly a strange Indian appeared and in a loud voice demanded that the woman explain her conduct. Was she selling her land to those *Evangelicos?* Wasn't it enough that he had cast a spell over her husband so that he couldn't talk? Did she want to have a worse spell cast over her? She could sell the land, but only to him.

This strange tirade in dialect from the Indians' most dreaded boss, the witch doctor, halted the sale and shattered the dream. Mr. Bundy and his committee sadly rolled up their measuring tape and went home. Weeks dragged into months, and then into years, and as the missionary noted the onion harvest on the desired lot, he wondered why the Lord did not intervene.

The years passed. Then came the years of the flood. Rains fell in torrential fury. At eleven o'clock one night in the lot the missionaries had hoped to buy, an irrigation ditch was filled to its usual height. Nearby a river roared between its banks. By six the following morning, that little ditch was ten feet deep and one hundred feet across as the nearby river swept along a new course.

If God had let the missionaries buy and build on that lot, every building, not to mention the topsoil, would have been swept away overnight. Who had prevailed: God or the witch doctor? In one night God had vindicated His "no" as an answer full of infinite wisdom.

"Can we thank the Lord beforehand for what He saves us from, as well as what He saves us to?" asks Mr. Bundy. "Let us trust more and worry less, that the glory be to God who doeth all things well."

Imagine two boys, at different times, asking their father for the use of the family car. One boy rushes in from a round of parties to say, "Dad, I am going to use the car tonight because I've got a date and there is no one who can take us where we want to go." To him, the father says, "I'm sorry, son. You cannot have the car tonight."

The other boy comes in with his father at the close of the day, from the field where they have been laboring together. The boy says, "Dad, if it suits you, I would like to use the car tonight." The father says, "Certainly, son, go ahead and use it."

The kind of prayer that helps Christians accomplish the impossible is the prayer that habitually identifies the purpose of the one who prays with God's purpose and thus is able in time of need to lay hold on God's power.

God answers prayer; sometimes, when hearts are weak.
He gives the very gifts believers seek.
But often faith must learn a deeper rest,
And trust God's silence when He does not speak;
For He whose name is Love will send the best.

Everyone That Asketh—Receiveth

I asked for strength that I might achieve.
He gave me weakness that I might learn obedience.
I asked for health that I might do great things.
He gave me sickness that I might do better things.
I asked for wealth that I might be happy.
He gave me poverty that I might be wise.
I asked for power that I might have glory.
He gave me impotence that I might realize my dependence
    upon Him.
I asked for all things that I might enjoy life.
He gave me life that I might enjoy things.
I received nothing that I asked for, but all I hoped for. I
    am rich; I am happy. My prayer is answered.

I know not by what methods rare,
But this I know, God answers prayer.
I know that He has given His Word,
Which tells me prayer is always heard,
And will be answered soon or late;
And so I pray and calmly wait.
I know not if the blessing sought
Will come in just the way I thought;
But leave my prayers with Him alone,
Whose will is wiser than my own,
Assured that He will grant my quest
Or send some answer far more blest.

Let us hear the conclusion of the whole matter: "Men ought always to pray, and not to faint." Even unanswered prayer teaches us this, being full, as so often it is, with unforeseen but wonderful blessings from Him who is the all-wise and the all-loving, "Fainting," says Dr. Hutton, "is falling backward; praying is falling forward. When we faint, we fall into abyss! When we pray, we fall upon God!" So . . .

> Be not afraid to pray—to pray is right
> Pray, if thou canst, with hope; but ever pray,
> Though hope be weak, or sick with long delay;
> Pray in the darkness, if there be no light . . .
> Whate'er is good to wish, ask that of Heaven,
> Though it be what thou canst not hope to see . . .
> But if for any wish thou darest not pray,
> Then pray to God to cast that wish away.

CHAPTER 8

Does God Always Come Through?

The truth is that we may not necessarily do a service to ourselves or to our Lord when we talk about only the good things the Lord does and the prayers He has obviously answered.

I was thrilled recently to hear the experience of a pilot who moved to our city; made a commitment to the Lord; hadn't been able to get a job; joined the First Baptist Church one Sunday; got a job offer on Monday; had a better one on Tuesday; and went to work as a commercial airplane pilot on Wednesday. That's good!

But I heard another story about an attorney, a fine Christian man. He may be about the most sterling character as a Christian man that I know, and he's had nothing but trouble in his law practice since he joined, and is wondering why.

I've stood in our pulpit and told some wonderful stories about people we prayed for who were instantly and divinely healed. But I've not told the stories of the folks we've prayed for who died. I know many testimonies of people who were saved and started to tithe and the next day got a raise. I love to tell those stories. But I also know stories about people who started to witness for Christ on the job and got fired.

Do things always work out? Does God always come to our rescue? Does every tragedy have a happy ending? Or, in fact, does God not always come through—in our understanding and from our perspective—after all?

God didn't rescue everybody in the Bible. God didn't come through for Moses—He let him die short of Jordan when he longed to go into the Promised Land more than anything else. Nor did He come through for Daniel, who had to spend time in a dungeon with the lions. He didn't come through for Job, but allowed Satan to bring calamity upon him.

God didn't come through for Joseph, but allowed him to be sold into slavery, beaten up by his brothers, thrown into a pit, left for dead, and cast into a dungeon for something he didn't do. Paul went to prison, John was banished to Patmos to live deserted and alone, and even God's own Son was left to die on a cross. No, God didn't spare them those experiences.

A Quaker philosopher once said, "It's no wonder God doesn't have any more friends, considering the way He treats the ones He already has." The fact of the matter is, the resounding answer to the question, "Does God Always Come Through?" is "no." *But while it's the fact of the matter, it's not the end of the issue.*

You remember from the third chapter of Daniel that King Nebuchadnezzar set up an image of himself, a golden idol, and said, "Now when the band starts to play, everybody is going to dance to my music. And when you hear it—morning, noon, and night—you must bow down, face the East, look at the idol, fall on your knees, and worship."

There were three young people, named Shadrach, Meshach, and Abednego, who said, "No. Our Lord is God. Jehovah is ours, and we will only worship Him." Nebuchadnezzar asked, "Is it true, O Shadrach, Meshach, and Abednego, do not ye serve my gods, nor worship the golden image which I have set up? . . . If ye worship not, ye shall be cast the same hour in the midst of a burning fiery furnace; and who is that God that shall deliver you out of my hands?" (Daniel 3:14–15). Shadrach, Meshach, and Abednego were three mature, upstanding believers. The answer they give is the most wholesome and mature psychological, emotional, and spiritual response to the problem of going through life's trials I have ever heard. We read it in Daniel 3:17:

"If it be so, our God whom we serve *is able* to deliver us."

Note especially the phrase "is able to deliver us." *"If it be so; if He wants to; if He gets good and ready, O king, He can deliver us out of the fire. We understand that! He is well able to do so and deliver us out of your hand."*

But see particularly the next three words in verse 18, *"But if not,* be it known unto thee, O king, that we will not serve thy gods, nor worship the golden image which thou hast set up."

The three young men went through the fire; had a glorious experience when it was finally over; and praised God in the midst of it because of two important attitudes: "Our God is *able* to keep us out of the trial. But if He doesn't, it isn't going to make any difference." Life is filled with "But if nots" for the believer.

There is a marvelous attitude here: He is able, but if He does not choose to do so, then it's all right. We're not going to cast away our faith and throw in the towel. We're going to keep playing the game anyway. We're going to keep loving Him and honoring Him and worshiping Him, like Job, who said, "Though he slay me, yet will I trust in him" (Job 13:15).

Ideally, philosophically, that sounds good. That would make a good sermon, and we could all say, "Amen. That's what the heroes of the faith do, and the way I would like to live." It's a neat trick if you can do it. But how? We must be aware of six things. There are six answers, six helps we must accept, believe, and live by if we are to have this kind of a philosophy and experientially begin to live as those heroes of faith did. When we pray for deliverance from the trial and no answer comes from God:

1. Remember the Proven Dependability of His Love. Not of His ways, not of His rescue attempts, but of His love—the proven dependability of it. Admittedly, God didn't always come through and rescue you out of the trial, but there are enough times when He *did* rescue you out of the trial to prove that He *does* love you. Doesn't Philippians 4:8 say, "Whatsoever things are true, whatsoever things are honest, whatsoever things are just, whatsoever things are pure, whatsoever things are lovely, whatsoever things are of good report; if there be any virtue, and if there be any praise, think on these things"?

Don't focus on the times you didn't get rescued. Every one of us has had enough good experiences to go with the bad to prove to us that He loves us. Many times God has taken the desperately awful and used it for good to prove He does love us and has our best interest at heart. He's proven His love enough times that we can keep believing He loves us even when He doesn't choose to show it in the same way as before.

In 1962 I had been traveling in evangelistic work without much opportunity to get home. I was leading a revival in the First Baptist Church, Salinas, California, and hadn't been home in six weeks. I wouldn't see my family again for three more weeks. I was going to Memphis the next Monday night to start a revival, and there was a plane leaving Los Angeles about 1:30 in the morning that stopped in Tulsa for six or seven hours to connect with another plane going to Memphis. I wanted desperately to catch that plane in Los Angeles.

The revival service in Salinas started early that Sunday night. Afterward, one of the church members drove me rather speedily about four or five hours to Los Angeles. Breathlessly I ran to catch that plane. As I raced to the gate, the door closed in my face. I was depressed and angry, to say the least. I checked into the airport hotel, gave the Lord a piece of my mind, and went to sleep.

The next morning I returned to the ticket counter to check in, stopped to have breakfast, and picked up the *Los Angeles Times*. The headlines announced that the very plane I had wanted to be on had collided with another flight over the Grand Canyon in one of the worst air tragedies in history, with more than 200 people killed. And I missed it by only a few seconds!

Today I can look back and remember the times that God revealed His mercy and proved how much He *did* love me to see me through a few times when, for His own purposes, things didn't work out as I would have liked. He doesn't have to come through in a way that we can see every time, but there is enough proof of His love that we can trust Him when He doesn't. So, even though I win some and lose some, I'm going to say, "My God is able, *but if not*, I'll serve Him."

2. Remember the Revelation of His Purpose. God has clearly revealed His purpose to us in the Scriptures. Romans 8:28 is one of the great verses in the Bible, but we cannot appreciate and claim it if we don't understand it in context. In verses 28 and 29 God reveals His purpose: "We know that all things work together for good to them that love God [the saved, the Christians; that's the promise of God to you] to them who are the called according to his purpose." And what is the purpose of God? He doesn't say purposes. God has only *one* main purpose in your life, and He accomplishes that purpose in many ways. "For whom he did foreknow, he also did predestinate." Why? What's the purpose of God? *"To be conformed to the image of his Son."*

Understand this—God wants you to become like

Jesus. He loves Jesus, and it seems He wants many more people like Jesus to love. The reason He saved you, came for you, and died for you is to make you like Jesus. But we have a long way to go to become like Him, don't we?

Immediately upon conversion, the process begins. God sees us as a big block of marble, and He knows somewhere down in there the Master Sculptor is going to carve out the image of His Son. It's in there somewhere, inside of us.

I think when the Lord sees how far He has to go, He must surely say, "I don't know where to start!" So He takes out His hammer and chisel; the hammer is difficulty, and the chisel is trial. And God says, "Well, the first thing wrong with this ol' boy is prejudice. I'm going to put him into the heat; I'm going to put him in the pressure cooker; I'm going to start chiseling away."

So He makes somebody move in next door to you whom you just can't stand. Now, you can change apartments the way some people change partners and jobs, and so move across town ten times, but they will keep on moving next door to you. And until you learn to love everybody—learn to become Christlike in that area of your life—He'll keep putting you through that particular trial.

Maybe your un-Christlike characteristic is faithlessness. You have to see everything by sight. You can't trust God for anything. You know what He'll do? He may take away every visible means of support. He may knock out all the props; He may bankrupt you; He may take everything away from you until you can't do anything *but* trust Him. He'll put you in that trial. "I'm going to chisel away at that piece," God will say, "till we make some progress, get closer to the image of My Son—a statue more like Jesus. Then I'll go to work on something else."

From beginning to end, from salvation to glorification, through trials and difficulties, the process of chiseling goes on. That's why understanding the revelation of God's purpose and His process in trying to make us like Jesus is so important. The process by which He does it is to put us in a pressure situation—a trial where something un-Christlike within us is dealt with.

3. *Remember the Sufficiency of His Grace.* God gives us the spiritual grit to do what we've got to do. That's called His grace. I am not speaking of the grace that means God gives us what we don't deserve. That's a different kind of grace. Rather, God will give us, in adequate measure, the grace we need to bear anything. How are we going to prove the grace of God—the adequacy of God to get us through hard times—if we never have any problems? First Corinthians 10:13 says, "There hath no temptation taken you but such as is common to man: but God is faithful, who will not suffer you to be tempted above that ye are able; but will with the temptation also make a way to escape, that ye may be able to bear it."

Let us see three important things about this verse. But first scratch out the word "temptation"—that's a poor Old English translation—and put in "trial." That being said, there are three things we must understand about the sufficiency of His grace. First, suffering is common to us all. The verse says, "There hath no trial taken you but such as is common to man." Every day I hear people say to me, "But you don't know what I'm going through." But I *do* know what they're going through. All of us on this pilgrim journey suffer. The names may change; the people who make us suffer may change; the figures or numbers involved may change; the situations, the circumstances, the dates vary, but everyone goes through the same things. It's only a matter of degree, and a matter of situation. But we all go through the same things. Paul says they are common to man.

Second, the apostle Paul writes, "God will not allow you to be tested above what you are able." You say, "Preacher, philosophically that sounds good—trust in

God; His grace will see you through anything, but the fact is I'm a human, and I've got a breaking point." Absolutely! And God knows where it is. If it is 14,836.1, He'll never let you go past 14,836.0. He'll bring you to the edge, but God knows the point beyond which you cannot stand any more, and He will not take you past that point.

Third, He says, "But He will, with the testing, with the trial, make a way of escape, that you may be able to bear it." You say, "A way of escape. Good! That means there's a way to get out of it." That is another poor Old English translation. The Greek word here interpreted "escape" doesn't mean "a way to get out of it." It means *"victory through the middle."*

How does a professional football team get to the Super Bowl? It involves suffering and coming against opposition. For instance, these dummy machines they push against only make the players tougher. We don't have victory without conflict—we don't have a hero without a war. No one is victorious without a battle. The trial makes us strong. And so God says the victory comes by going *through* the trial. Don't try to elude all struggle. Draw deeply upon God's grace, believe in His adequacy, trust Him, and go through it.

And I want to remind you that I don't think God owes us an answer and has to explain "why" in everything that happens. He has proven that He loves us enough in the times that He did give us a "why" that we can trust Him in the times the answers don't come. His grace is more than sufficient.

4. *Remember the Mystery of His Ways.* Remember that there is a big difference in the *acts* of God and the *ways* of God. The average person interprets what God is and what He is up to by His acts. But the spiritually mature person interprets the acts of God in light of the mysterious *ways* of God. The ways of God are past finding out. Remember Isaiah 55:8–9: "My thoughts are not your

thoughts, *neither are your ways my ways, . . .* For as the heavens are higher than the earth, so are *my ways higher than your ways."*

We mentioned the time when the fiery serpents were biting the children of Israel. Had they been a contemporary church, the Israelites would have organized a Committee for the Extermination of Reptiles. But that's not God's way. He says, "Just let them bite." The *act* of God was that the snakes were allowed to bite; but the *way* of God was to raise a solution in the midst of the pollution—not wipe out pollution—thereby teaching them to have great faith. God said, "Here is the answer; here's a brazen serpent. Whosoever looks will be healed and live." Why? Because He wanted the people to learn to believe.

People ask, "Why didn't God kill Hitler?" "Why doesn't God kill the drug dealers?" "Why doesn't God stamp out sin?" That's not God's way because man has a free will. That's God's great gift to man, it is what makes him in the image of God. It is God's way to raise up a cure for us to look at by faith, in the form of an old rugged cross.

To Israel, God revealed His mighty acts; only to Moses did He reveal His ways. It was the act of the Roman governor that put Paul in prison; it was the way of God to put him in prison so he could experience God's grace and write his great treatise on the sufficiency and adequacy of that grace. It was God's act to let an innocent old man be exiled on the island of Patmos; it was the way of God to put him there to have the time and isolation he needed to receive the entire Revelation of St. John. It was God's act to let His Son die on the cross; it was the way of God to redeem the world through that act. So don't interpret God by His *acts*, but try to have a comprehension of *the mystery of His ways.*

5. *Get a Good Appreciation for the Nature of His Person.* Learn to delight more in *who God is* than in *what*

God does. Now, how can we do that? First, we begin to comprehend the mystery of His ways. We interpret what happens in His revealed purpose through trials to bring us to maturity. We draw on the sufficiency of His grace. We concentrate on the proven dependability of His love when He did choose to come through. In so doing, we learn to take delight in who the Lord *is*, not just in what He is doing.

If our spiritual thermometers rise and fall based only on what's currently happening in our lives, we will lose the value of going through a trial for our own good. If our spiritual thermometers are down and we're down on God, we won't keep Him in focus to see what He's up to. Life will then be a roller coaster—hot and cold; up and down—and a constant frustration. The acts of God change, but His ways don't. What God *does* changes; what God *is* changes not. Rejoice in Him who is changeless.

One day the disciples rejoiced because the demons were subject to them. Jesus told them not to rejoice in that, rather to rejoice because their names were written down in heaven.

Why? Because Jesus knew there would be times when the disciples' attempts at exorcism would fail. He didn't want them feeling up and down when circumstances were up and down. "Rejoice in something that doesn't change," He said, "Rejoice in the constant, fixed, changeless nature of your relationship with God—that changes not."

6. *Remember the Promise of His Tomorrow.* Does God always come through? No, not that we see. But yes, ultimately. We're not living our lives in isolation. We touch those who have gone before and those who will come after. We are human beings in the world, in a school, in a society, in a home, but all of that is subject to the fact that first and foremost we are citizens of the greater kingdom of God. And all of that, we have seen by the Book, turns out right.

As we pass through "trials" that don't go away, as we pray for answers that don't come, let us remember the three Hebrew children whose attitude was, "He can, but if He doesn't, we'll still love Him and worship Him and trust Him and serve Him." What happened to them? He didn't rescue them. They got thrown into the fiery furnace, heated up seven times. But when the guards opened the door to check on them, there was a fourth man in the fire, *like unto the Son of God.*

Better to be in the furnace with Jesus, than on the outside looking in without Him. Trust Him.

God answers every prayer. Sometimes His answer is "yes"; sometimes it is "no"; sometimes it is "wait." Let us trust Him and praise Him no matter what the answer.

CHAPTER 9

Praying for Healing

At the heart of the Charismatic movement is an emphasis on two gifts originally intended as signs to unbelievers: the gift of speaking in languages not learned and the gift of healing.

It is difficult to fault anyone who wants to see another healed and is doing everything he can to make it happen. Our hearts go out quite naturally to the sick and the suffering. No one wants to see a child sick, a marriage wrecked, a heart broken, a teenager crippled, or an adult stricken with cancer. Suffering, sickness, and disease are the plight of the human race, and deep in the heart of the believer is an empathy for those who long with all their hearts to see those ills annihilated.

It is not the purpose of this chapter to destroy the faith of people who long to see God work in restoring health to their loved ones. Someone has suggested that we should never offer negative teaching on this subject lest we uproot the faith of those who would believe, which believing might produce healing. We must argue conversely that it is more damaging to hold out false hope to those in whose lives healing will never come.

There is a great need in the Christian body to look objectively at the truth of Scripture and attempt to discern what is and what is not provided in the atonement of Christ in regard to physical health.

Some time ago I was called to the home of a church member to pray for a seventeen-year-old girl at the point of death from cancer. Upon arriving, I was surprised to find that two prominent Charismatic teachers from our city had also been called. After a few minutes of reading the Bible, laying on hands, and prayer, we rose to leave. The Charismatic teachers assured the girl that she would absolutely be healed, that healing was provided for by the atonement on the cross, and that she soon would begin to recover. In less than sixty days we conducted the girl's funeral. Today her parents have survived that difficult experience with the help of God and have found Him whose grace is sufficient to be their strength and their confidence. With gladness and faith they look forward to the great morning of resurrection when their daughter, with all saints, will receive her new glorified body—"when we shall be like Him, for we shall see Him as He is."

One cannot help but wonder, though her parents survived the ordeal and grew stronger by it, how many thousands of people have been harmed and their faith in God destroyed because such strong assurances were given by Charismatics whose guarantee never came to fruition. God does heal—let there be no question about that. But not in every case. Sometimes there is healing, and sometimes there is not.

I have come to understand through the years that God is not accountable to us. We answer to Him and not vice versa. God does not have to answer to us, and the truth is—all the Charismatic books, promises, sermons, theologies, prayer cloths, and healing lines to the contrary notwithstanding—that sometimes God heals in answer to prayer and sometimes He doesn't. The stock Charismatic answer to this dilemma (through some moderate Charismatics demur), is that God always heals unless there is not enough faith and/or unless there is sin. With this we vehemently disagree. Some of the greatest saints I know—people who have fantastic faith and live lives as nearly perfect as one may live—are terribly twisted by disease and are never healed. Why? I don't know, and nobody else knows. Only heaven will reveal the answer to that question. Until then, God's only answer is, "My grace is sufficient for thee."

Are Charismatics on track when they say that God is bound to heal when two ingredients are present: (1) righteousness, or absence of sin, and (2) the presence of faith? Stated another way, is the only reason why God does not heal in answer to prayer the presence of sin or the lack of faith? The answer is "no." The Charismatics are off track. The ultimate answer is, as is always the case, the sovereignty of God.

In the Gospel of John three incidents of healing are recorded. Are the ingredients of personal righteousness and faith present in them all? Indeed they are not. In John 4 we read of the healing of the nobleman's son. In John 5, there is the healing of the impotent man at the Pool of Bethesda. In John 9 we are told of the healing of the man born blind.

In the first instance there is no personal faith or righteousness indicated in the life of the boy who was healed. The lad was at the point of death, probably unconscious or possibly in a coma. The gentile nobleman was very likely not a believer, nor was his son. Jesus answered strictly out of compassion. The nobleman besought Jesus for the healing; that is, he begged Him or entreated Him earnestly. The only factor present was strong desire. Nothing is spoken of the man's faith or righteousness, and it's unlikely that the nobleman possessed either. Certainly none could be exhibited in the life of an unconscious boy. The only ingredients present were the man's desire and the Savior's compassion.

In the case of the impotent man it was not personal righteousness or faith that brought the healing, but rather the compassion of the Savior expressed in the sovereignty of God. Jesus did not ask the man if he was righteous or had faith to be well. The only question was, "Do you want to be well?" (John 5:6). Still the man had no faith in Christ. His only faith was in the water of the pool; his pitiful response was, "I have no man to put me into the pool." Jesus then said, "Rise, take up thy bed, and walk." Verse 9 records, "Immediately the man was made whole." The man's rising was not an act of faith that made him whole. His rising was the response to the healing. The grace of God had made him whole. Jesus healed the man on the spot, and only *after* he was made whole did he take up his bed and walk.

In John Jesus makes it clear that in the case of the man born blind neither sin in his life nor sin in his parents had anything to do with the man's problem or its solution. It was *allowed* within the sovereignty of God in order to reveal His glory. In this case there was faith: the man was told to do something to be healed. He believed Jesus and did what he was told and gained sight.

In none of these three cases in John is personal righteousness indicated as a factor in the healing. In only one instance—that of the blind man—is faith required. In the case of the nobleman's son faith is at best possibly only inferred in the heart of the father. It is clear that the impotent man had no faith at all. So if personal righteousness and faith are not the common denominators in these healings, what is? Plainly the sovereignty of a God who does *as* He wills *when* He wills in order to reveal His glory.

During my pastoral ministry I have been called twelve or fifteen times to go to the home of people who were sick, anoint them with oil, and pray for them. In each case I responded affirmatively and compassionately. I once saw a fever drop from 104 degrees to 98.6 degrees in a moment. I once saw carbuncles fall from the arms and hands of a woman. At other times I felt the same leading, followed the same procedure, but nothing happened. In the young girl's case I never felt more strongly that God was leading and that she was being healed. One Sunday morning our entire church prayed for her, and the whole audience seemed to glow with a "white presence." But still she died. The answer? There is no answer.

Through the years I have come to a theological position that has helped me. On the one hand, the Charismatics often offer hope to people that is not valid, has no theological base, and is proved by experience not to be real. On the other hand, my fellow Baptists often go to the opposite extreme and never pray for anyone except under two conditions: (1) It is Wednesday night and not Sunday; and (2) if they are not in church, but somewhere else. The reason for this posture is very likely that we have overreacted against the Charismatics and have no theological basis for answering the question, "Why doesn't it happen all the time?"

Through the years, therefore, I have come to believe that the best thing to do is pray for all sick people all the time to get well and to pray with all the faith we know how. *If God answers, praise His name! If He doesn't answer, praise Him anyway!* While it is true that God apparently never intends to heal all the people the Charismatics would have us to believe, it is also probably true that God would like to heal many more than He does if we would only pray and give Him the chance.

Undoubtedly healing was the sign gift used most often by our Lord. There are three categories of spiritual gifts: the gifts bestowed on gifted men and women; sign gifts to unbelievers; and gifts to edify the body of Christ. Among the sign gifts are miracles, exorcism, languages, and healing.

It should be understood that New Testament healing was given only to unsaved people, most of whom believed in Christ in response to this miraculous sign.

James, the brother of Jesus, admonishes in his epistle that if anyone is sick, he should call for the elders of the church to pray for him. He does not say, "Call for the healer, or the one with the gift of healing." It is the ministry of the church to pray for its members who are sick. Often through prayer, through medicine, through proper diet, and even through the miraculous, Christians will be healed. But it is not because someone with a gift for healing has confronted them. If anyone today has the gift of healing, then let him get out of his tent, out of his TV studio, or out of his professional environment and get into the slums of Calcutta and New Delhi and walk up and down the streets saying to the sick and dying—as did our Lord and His servant, Peter—"Take up thy bed and walk." To the conviction that God heals, we say "yes"; that men have the gift of healing, we say "no."

Recently it was my sad responsibility to minister to a young couple who had just lost a two-year-old child. Nearly as sad as the loss of the child was the struggle they were having because well-meaning Charismatics had only recently come, prayed in tongues, and assured them that the child was healed and would live. When they anointed with oil and prayed, they assured the couple that if they did not have enough faith, *God would have perfect faith for them.* This unscriptural precept had raised false hopes and left the parents in a condition that greatly strained their faith in God.

For this reason, we would do well, therefore, to attempt to discern precisely what James's teaching on the subject does and and does not mean.

> Is any among you afflicted? let him pray. Is any merry? let him sing psalms. Is any sick among you? let him call for the elders of the church; and let them pray over him, anointing him with oil in the name of the Lord: And the prayer of faith shall save the sick, and the Lord shall raise him up; and if he has committed sins, they shall be forgiven him. Confess your faults

one to another, and pray one for another, that ye may be healed. The effectual fervent prayer of a righteous man availeth much. *James 5:13–16*

The background of this teaching is that mankind in general and Jews in particular have always believed that sickness and suffering are somehow related to sin. The Book of Job was written in part to say that such is not the case. But the idea persists to this very day. We remember only too well the question of the Pharisees to Jesus, "Who sinned, this boy or his parents, that he was born blind?" It is explicit in James's text that some sickness is indeed the direct result of sin and some is not. Moreover, when Jesus healed the paralytic lowered through the roof by his friends, He first forgave his sins (Luke 5:18–20). At other times He healed diseases, particularly congenital ones, without dealing with sin. *Keep in mind that some sickness is caused directly by sin and some is not.*

When sin is the immediate cause, it must be confessed and forsaken before the illness can be remitted. On many occasions when Jesus healed, He said, "Thy faith hath saved thee," indicating that in those cases, physical healing and spiritual salvation occurred simultaneously.

A study of the Greek text in James's passage indicates he is dealing with two kinds of sickness on different bases. James 5:13 asks, "Is any afflicted among you?" The Greek word for afflicted is *"kakopatheo"*—*"kako,"* meaning "evil" or "bad," and *"patheo,"* from which we get "pathology," meaning "physical."

In verse 14 James asks, "Are there any sick?" The word for "sick" is *astheneo,* meaning "under the weather for any reason." There is no moral possibility in this word *"astheneo,"* though there is in *kakopatheo,* translated "afflicted."

James is obviously dealing with two kinds of sicknesses. The man who is sick without any morally related absolute is to call for the church to pray over and with

77

him. And if he incidentally has committed sins, they will also be forgiven. But the man who has been afflicted with *"kakopatheo"*—who is pathologically ill, related to his moral weakness—is to pray for himself. Again, there is no moral quality in the word for "sick," though there may have been sins in the man's life not related to the sickness, which also would be forgiven incidental to the healing.

The Greek word for "save the sick" in verse 15 is *sozo*, meaning "spiritual salvation related to the saving of the soul." It seems obvious from James's vocabulary that he intended to contrast this kind of situation with another kind to which he was referring in the use of the word *kakopatheo*, translated "afflicted," in which the physical malady was related to sin. This *sozo* kind of sickness must be dealt with by the ill person himself by confessing his sins. The man with the sickness that is not sin-related is allowed to call for help from the elders of the church. But James's instruction to the man with the sin-related sickness in verse 13 is, "Let him pray." This man must deal personally with the sin that has caused his sickness. No one can help him in that. He is responsible to deal before God with his own sin. The promise of help from the church, and the only case in which anointing and group prayer is commanded, appears also to be in the case of an innocent child or a nearly perfect saint.

The general thesis of this Scripture passage is that sickness can be related to sin, for in verse 16 James sums it all up by saying, "Acknowledge your sins one to another, and pray one for another that you may be healed."

In 5:17 James closes the subject with a marvelous illustration of the truth he has been stating—that disease can be related to evil, but is not always. To illustrate when it is related, he reminds us of Elijah and his praying. Of all the possible illustrations, why did James use the story of Elijah? For years, King Ahab and Queen Jezebel had led the children of Israel into idolatry and Baal worship. The result of this sin was drought upon the land (1 Kings

16:33–17:1). When revival came, the rain returned, and the malady of the physical sickness of the land was removed (1 Kings 18:42–45).

In a sentence, James is saying there are two kinds of sickness. Some sickness is the direct result of sin. In such cases, the person must deal by himself with his sin for the sickness to go away. But sometimes sickness is not directly the result of sin. Though the sickness may not be the result of specific sin, however, we are still all sinners. In these cases we may call for help from the church, and in the process, sin will be forgiven incidentally (v. 15). James does not say that the primary result of this corporate prayer is that the man will be well. Rather, the Lord will forgive his sins: "saving the sick man," which means salvation from sin. It may be the case, however, that there will be physical healing as well. But the promise of healing in the Epistle of James deals with only *some* sickness—that caused by sin.

It should further be said that healing is *not* in the atonement. When Charismatics say, "Healing is in the atonement," they mean that on the same basis of Christ's death on the cross by which we can claim instant forgiveness of sin, any believer can claim instant healing from sickness.

It is a theology that sounds good on the surface and may appear superficially to have some biblical support, but I have noticed that *when my Charismatic friends get sick, they conveniently drop out of the church for a while and don't show up until they are well again.* Jesus died for our sicknesses as well as our sins. Some even teach He died two deaths on the cross: one for sickness, one for sin. Yet the apostle Peter writes, "He died once for all" (1 Peter 3:18). (See also Hebrews 7:27.)

God created a perfect world in which nature was in harmony with itself and with God. Man's body was in perfect health. Man was at peace with the animals, with his environment, his universe, himself, his fellowman, and his God. Sin changed everything. Because of sin the soul lost fellowship with God and was destined for hell. Because of sin man was out of sorts with his fellowman. The body of his flesh fell under the condemnation of God and began to die. Everything in man's world came under the curse of God as a result of the first sin.

How, then, should we regard "healing in the atonement" in light of the Fall? Consider the following: Jesus tells us in Luke 21:28 that when we see the signs of the end of the age, we are to "Look up, . . . for your redemption *draweth nigh.*" The apostle Peter, however, writes in his first epistle, "Ye know that ye *were* not redeemed with corruptible things, as silver and gold, . . . But with the precious blood of Christ" (1:18–19). On the one hand, Jesus tells us that at His future coming we *will be redeemed.* Peter tells us that back at the cross we already *have been redeemed.* What has *been* redeemed, and what is *to be* redeemed?

The soul has been saved. The precious soul of the sinner has already been redeemed—but that is all. The redemption of the soul from sin was provided by the Cross and Resurrection and is past tense. The redemption of everything else is provided by Christ's glorious return, when He makes all things new, and is future tense. This is the theme of the entire Book of Revelation.

The Charismatics are off in their timing. They are sincere, but on this point they are poor theologians. Their hearts are right, but their timetable is wrong.

Paul writes, "We have this treasure [the salvation of the soul] in earthen vessels" (2 Corinthians 4:7). The precious treasure of heavenly salvation deposited in us by the Holy Spirit indwells an earthly body that is under the curse of sin and death, subject to sin, sickness, disease, and death, whose complete redemption is a future event—"To wit, the redemption of our body" (Romans 8:23). When the end of the world begins and Christ returns in glory, then we are to "look up, for our redemption is near."

At the resurrection and rapture of Christians living and dead—and only then—will we receive our glorified bodies and be in perfect health. Then, and then alone, will the believer have restored access to the perfect health provided in the Garden of Eden in his original, perfect state before the Fall. When our Lord returns, He will set up His kingdom on earth, and righteousness will cover the earth as the waters cover the sea. Only then will there be peace on earth. There will be a thousand years of peace under the government of Jesus Christ in fulfillment of Isaiah's prophecy, "And the government shall be upon his shoulder" (9:6). Only then will the animal kingdom be redeemed. The animals have been affected by sin; every animal has its natural enemy; animals kill other animals. But then the wolf shall lie down with the lamb (11:6). At the end of the Millennium the earth and the universe, which are still under the curse of sin, shall be redeemed. Paul writes,

> For we know that the whole creation groaneth and travaileth in pain together until now. And not only they, but ourselves also, which have the first fruits of the Spirit, even we ourselves groan within ourselves, waiting for the adoption, to wit, the redemption of our body. *Romans 8:22–23*

Peter tells us,

> But the day of the Lord will come as a thief in the night; in which the heavens shall pass away with a great noise, and the elements shall melt with fervent heat, the earth also and the works that are therein shall be burned up. Seeing then that all these things shall be dissolved, what manner of persons ought ye to be in all holy conversation and godliness, Looking for and hasting unto the coming of the day of God, wherein the heavens being on fire shall be dissolved, and the elements shall melt with fervent heat? *2 Peter 3:10–12*

John added,

> And I saw a new heaven and a new earth: for the first
> heaven and the first earth were passed away; and there
> was no more sea. And I John saw the holy city, new
> Jerusalem, coming down from God out of heaven,
> prepared as a bride adorned for her husband. *Revelation
> 21:1–2*

Our Lord's promise "Behold, I make all things new"
will come to fruition, but only in God's perfect time. It is
important to note in careful Bible study that *when* God
does something is often as important as *what* God does.
Jesus did not die one death for sin, one for our diseased
bodies, one for society, one for the animals, one for the
earth, and one for the universe. He will ultimately restore
a perfect earth in a perfect universe indwelled by perfect
men in perfect bodies, but *that* provision is made in His
future glorious return when He makes all things new.

We should consider several problem verses that the
Charismatics claim as proof texts for "healing on demand."
Their favorite may well be,

> But he was wounded for our transgressions, he was
> bruised for our iniquities: the chastisement of our
> peace was upon him; and with his stripes we are
> healed. *Isaiah 53:5*

I have not found one classical theologian or historic
Bible scholar or commentator who does not agree that in
context this verse refers to healing from sin. There is no
discussion of the healing of the body in Isaiah 53. The
chapter pictures the sinner as having the sickness of sin in
the totality of his being, with wholeness provided in the
death of a sufficient Messiah. To attempt to read physical
healing into this passage is a gross transgression of every
time-honored hermeneutical principle.

> When the even was come, they brought unto him
> many that were possessed with devils: and he cast out

the spirits with his word, and healed all that were sick:
That it might be fulfilled which was spoken by Esaias
the prophet, saying, Himself took our infirmities, and
bare our sicknesses. *Matthew 8:16–17*

A careful examination of the text makes it clear that
Jesus was not just healing the sick, but also casting out
demons, that He Himself might take our infirmities and
sickness away. Jesus did not heal, pray, preach, suffer
ridicule, rejection, and death without entering into
empathy with sinful, sick, rejected, dying mankind. He
felt what we feel. He was not a cold stoic who healed the
suffering and oppressed by some magic, unfeeling wave of a
theological wand. He empathizes with us. He feels with us.
He hurts with us. He suffers with us. He weeps with us. It
is that sense in which He came in fulfillment of prophecy
to die for His people. He did not die for our diseases. He
died for our sins.

Matthew is saying that Jesus did all this in fulfillment
of Isaiah's prophecy. The manner of life Jesus lived was the
kind the prophet Isaiah said the Messiah would live. *At this
point in Matthew, Jesus had not died yet. It is impossible that
this experience in Matthew 8 is a picture of Jesus carrying our
diseases by His death, for He had not yet died.* Matthew's
statement is prophetical, not theological. Had the words,
"Christ bore our sicknesses," appeared in the theological
epistles such as Romans, Ephesians, or Galatians, we
might hold a different view. But Matthew's purpose was to
show that *even before He died,* Jesus was acting out the kind
of earthly ministry that was prophesied for the Messiah.

The apostle Paul's summation of the gospel is in
1 Corinthians 15:1–3. It is significant that not one word
of healing occurs and that the death of Christ was for
sickness as well as sin. His epistle to the Romans is the
ultimate work on the nature and purpose of Christ's
atoning work of salvation; interestingly, it says not one
word about physical healing. If healing were as important a

part of the gospel of redemption as Charismatics say, Paul would have mentioned it in this great treatise.

Another favorite Charismatic verse is,

> Who his own self bare our sins in his own body on the tree, that we, being dead to sins, should live unto righteousness: by whose stripes ye were healed. For ye were as sheep going astray. . . . *1 Peter 2:24*

Careful study shows another prophetic fulfillment of the nature of the empathic Christ. There are no references to healing in any verses around this passage. Peter wrote, "Ye were healed," not "Ye are being healed." Moreover, Peter says we *were* redeemed by the precious blood of Christ, and Jesus says our redemption is *still in the future*. It is obvious that Peter means our souls have been healed from the sickness of sin as our bodies are yet to be healed from the sickness of disease.

Peter further indicates that suffering is in accordance with the will of God. There is no question that God allows suffering of all kinds to come upon His children for two purposes: (1) To rebuke and chastise with a remedial view in mind; and (2) to allow them to glorify Him and, like Paul, testify to the sufficiency of His grace. First Peter 3:14–17 says that we ought to be happy when we suffer for righteousness' sake, but unhappy when we suffer for doing evil.

> But and if ye suffer for righteousness' sake, happy are ye: and be not afraid of their terror, neither be troubled; But sanctify the Lord God in your hearts: and be ready always to give an answer to every man that asketh you a reason of the hope that is in you with meekness and fear: Having a good conscience; that, whereas they speak evil of you, as of evildoers, they may be ashamed that falsely accuse your good conversation in Christ. For it is better, if the will of God be so, that ye suffer for well-doing, than for evil-doing.

Peter says again in 4:16–19,

Yet if any man suffer as a Christian, let him not be ashamed; but let him glorify God on this behalf. For the time is come that judgment must begin at the house of God: and if it first begin at us, what shall the end be of them that obey not the gospel of God? And if the righteous scarcely be saved, where shall the ungodly and the sinner appear? Wherefore let them that suffer according to the will of God commit the keeping of their souls to him in well-doing, as unto a faithful Creator.

We who "suffer according to the will of God" commit the keeping of our souls to God. We must not bite the hand that feeds us. We must not criticize the One who tries us for our own good and turn on the One who has allowed the suffering for our benefit. The structure of the Greek text makes it imperative that it is not our *response* to the suffering that is according to His will, *but the suffering itself.*

As stated earlier, there are no specific instances of Christians being healed in the New Testament. The purpose of the gift was always to convince unbelievers when it was exercised upon them. Christians need no such sign. Paul needed no sign of languages at his conversion or filling because he already believed; neither did he need the sign of healing. Therefore, God's answer to his prayer for the deliverance of his "thorn in the flesh" was "My grace is sufficient for thee." Paul did not heal Timothy when he was sick, but told him rather, "Use a little wine for thy stomach's sake and thine often infirmities" (1 Timothy 5:23). Neither did Paul heal his colaborer, Trophimus, but left him sick at Miletus (2 Timothy 4:20).

What happens when the Charismatic doctrine of "healing on demand" is carried to its ultimate possibility? If all sickness, all ill health, all physical malady can be healed instantly in answer to prayer on the basis of Christ's atonement, how do we deal with the fact that ultimately everyone dies of something? The Charismatic's pathetic answer to this question is that in such an instance we gain control of our death. We decide our own destiny. We "will" to die and simply allow death to take us, deciding when we will to depart this earthly life. *That is heresy of the first order!* It implies that we are, in effect, becoming God ourselves, for only Jesus was able to do that on the cross. He willed His death and the precise moment of it. "No man can take my life," He said, "I lay it down willingly."

Our God heals today. Sometimes He heals through medicine; sometimes through prayer; and sometimes through the patient awaiting of the glorified body at resurrection. But He does heal.

Our loving God answers the prayers of His children. He heals the sick bodies of all who belong to Him. Again, it is only a matter of His glorious time schedule. The issue becomes not *whether* He heals, but *when* He heals. In heaven, the physical body, which has been sown in corruption, is raised in incorruption–a glorified, perfect body like unto His own. No such perfect health is ever promised the unbeliever.

If it is true, as Charismatics insist, that healing is for everyone in all cases here and now because "healing is in the atonement," we could claim instant healing on the basis of Christ's death on the cross the same as we could claim instant forgiveness from sin. If we so much as call the doctor or even take an aspirin when we are sick, we are insulting the finished work of Calvary. This action is an affront to the Cross, and our very acts belie what we say we believe. We add nothing to the work of the Cross to gain remission of sin. Why do we add to it to gain healing from sickness? It means we do not believe what we say we believe. Good works are the result of the forgiveness of sin, not a part of it.

CHAPTER 10

When Does God Heal?

What does the Word of God have to say as to His will for us in the matter of healing? His revelations in this respect are both *general* and *specific*.

We have the general promises of deliverance, protection, and provision that we have only to apply to the particular circumstances of our own lives in order to ask within the limits of the revealed will of God.

But there are also specific revelations.

For instance, 1 Corinthians 13:10 tells us that it is God's will that we should not yield to temptation, and a promise is given of sufficient grace to overcome. In such an hour, therefore, when praying for strength, it would be foolish and a dishonor to God to say, "If it be Thy will."

The same thing is true in James 1:5 with regard to the prayer for wisdom. It is likewise true in John 6:40, in 2 Peter 3:9, and in John 5:16 with regard to the salvation of souls.

A certain healing evangelist says, "No one would think of praying, 'O God, save my child; nevertheless if it be Thy will that my child be lost forever, Thy will, O God, and not mine be done.'"

In this he is quite right. The very thought of such a prayer is repellent. It would be a slander on God's love, an arrogant denial of His word, and an insult to His honor.

But on whose authority do the "healing" people place the removal of sickness in this life in the same relationship to the will of God as that which the Word of God does for the salvation for the soul in the life to come?

Where is it said in the Word of God that "it is *always* the will of God to heal *all* who have need of healing"?

Where has it been revealed in God's Word that it is His will for His children always in each and every particular instance to remain in unimpaired health?

Unless there is a revelation above and beyond the Word, how can we as a rule pray acceptably for the sick unless we say, "Thy will, O God, not mine, be done"?

Does it not often hold true that the finest saints are the greatest sufferers? Is it not often the case that those whose lives have given the most crystalline evidence of the profoundest spirituality and closest fellowship with God have been the very ones called upon to endure the greatest pain and the deepest suffering?

Is this chargeable to lack of faith, to spiritual inability to rightly discern at the table of Communion the Lord's body broken for the healing of their diseases, or perhaps to some unconfessed sin in their lives?

God pity us if we must so conclude!

Was there ever a choicer saint of God than Fanny Crosby, the blind hymn writer? We marvel at the soul of this woman, and we are constrained to say, "Behold what her affliction hath wrought!" Who knows but that with two good eyes she might have glorified God less. It would be difficult to conceive how she could have glorified Him more. Here is what she wrote:

> *Yielded to God, my body, soul, and spirit,*
> *Oh, what rejoicing fills my peaceful breast;*
> *All, all is well, no doubt nor fear disturbs me,*

> *While on His promise now alone I rest.*
> *Yielded to God, and in His holy keeping,*
> *My heart His temple evermore shall be;*
> *Yielded to God, in willing consecration,*
> *Blessed Redeemer, I am lost in Thee.*

Thus yielded, body, soul, and spirit, and yet *blind.* Why?

I venture to say there has not been a Christian in all the word mightier in prayer, more devoted, more Spirit-filled and enlightened than the apostle Paul. Why, then, did this mighty man of prayer have to leave Trophimus sick at Miletus (2 Timothy 4:20)? Why did Paul's prayers not avail to raise him up? Why were the prayers of this man of mountain-moving faith not availing to heal Epaphroditus *immediately,* as all who came to Jesus while He was here on earth were healed (Philippians 2:25–27)?

Why did this holy man, to whom the "deep things of God" were revealed, have to advise Timothy to take a little wine for his stomach's sake? And why did Timothy, who "from a child knew the holy scriptures," have to endure his *"often* infirmities"? (See 1 Timothy 5:23.)

Why did this man, who revealed to us so much of the knowledge of the ways of God, this bondservant of Christ, who loved his Master unto death—why did he have to earnestly pray three times for "the thorn in his flesh" to be removed, only to be told by the Lord that it was better for him to endure it (2 Corinthians 12:8–9)?

Why, we ask again, unless it was that in these particular instances it was not the will of God that the sick ones should be healed?

Dr. R. A. Torrey put it well when he wrote,

> The antecedent probability in any given case is in favor of healing; *for health is the general will of God for His people.* But one may need a "thorn in his flesh," "a messenger of Satan," just as the Apostle did, to keep him humble. In such cases no amount of praying, nor

of anointing either for that matter, will bring healing. In Paul's case the physical infirmity is allowed of God; *it is His gift*, with the gracious purpose of keeping the sick one humble in the midst of many revelations.

Where did Paul get this "thorn" that so irritated his "flesh" as to cause him to pray so earnestly for its removal? It is said distinctly that it was "given to him." Someone, therefore, gave it to him.

It was given for a *holy purpose*—that he might not "be exalted above measure through the abundance of the revelations" with which he had been honored (2 Corinthians 12:7).

If the affliction was given to Paul for such a purpose— to keep him humble, to enrich him spiritually, and thus to be better fitted for the testimony he was to leave to the world—then here is one infirmity we may be sure was not given by the hand of the Devil.

After being told that he must be satisfied to endure the thorn, but that Christ's grace would be sufficient for him, Paul said, "Most gladly therefore will I glory in my infirmities, that the power of Christ may rest upon me" (2 Corinthians 12:9).

Paul testifies that, by and through his infirmity— whatever its particular nature may have been—the spiritual power of the Son of God was to rest on him.

Do you in all honor and honesty think that the Devil ever operates for a purpose like this?

Where, then, did Paul get his "thorn in the flesh"? Who could have given it to him under such circumstances but the Lord Himself?

As far as this affliction is concerned, God tells the apostle that it is better for him to bear his infirmity than to be rid of it.

Our healing brethren would have us believe that the author of all sickness is the Devil. One has said, "Every sickness, disease, and deformity, which Christ cured while on earth, was the result of Satan's work, and it is the same today." One leaflet called "Do You Know God's Way of Healing?" says still more:

> *Question:* "Do you mean to say that *all* disease is Satan's work?"
>
> *Answer:* "Yes, for if there had been no sin (which came through Satan) there never would have been any disease."
>
> *Question:* "But does disease never come from God?"
>
> *Answer:* "No, it cannot come from God, for He is pure, and disease is unclean; and it cannot come out of heaven, for there is no disease there."

But what do these who so teach have to say about 2 Samuel 12:15, which says, "And the Lord [not the Devil] struck the child . . . and it was very sick"?

What will they say of 2 Kings 15:5, which says, "And the Lord [not the Devil] smote the king, so that he was a leper unto the day of his death"?

Let us consider what God's Word really says about the matter.

1. If the Devil is really the author of all disease, then of course there could have been no sickness or disease during the period of man's innocency, however brief or long that period may have been.

The above-mentioned leaflet states, "If there had been no sin [of which the Devil ever has been and is the author], there never would have been any disease." But is this assumption, or is it Scripture?

Would it have been impossible for the first man to catch cold had he subjected himself to the physical conditions that bring it about? Suppose a huge rock or a mighty tree trunk had fallen on this man and crushed his body—do you not think that his quivering flesh would have been filled with the most intense pain and suffering?

Even if it be granted that physical death came

through the breach of the moral law, is it not true, as R. V. Bingham says in his splendid little volume, *The Bible and the Body*, "It is possible that in the unfallen creation there were things that man might do without breach of moral law, which might lead to derangement of physical laws"?

Is it sound logic to say that all the present physical ills are traceable in any moral sense to sin? What did Jesus mean by His reply to the questioning disciples concerning the man blind from his birth? They asked, "Master, who did sin, this man or his parents, that he was born blind?"

Jesus answered, "Neither hath this man sinned, nor his parents: but that the works of God should be made manifest in him" (John 9:2–3).

There is, according to R. V. Bingham, "a tremendous amount of sickness in the world today which has no direct connection with sin, and, as far as the individual sufferer is concerned, is due to no breach of the Moral law."

2. Once more, in claiming that the Devil is the author of all disease, our well-meaning but misguided friends utterly confuse the penalty for sin with the sin itself. The Devil *is* the author of the sin, but in a very certain sense it is God who is the author of the penalty. It was God, not the Devil, who said, "In the day thou eatest thereof thou shalt surely die." It was God, not the Devil, who said, "The soul that sinneth it shall die."

The author of a crime is not the author of the penalty affixed to the crime. The criminal is the author of the crime. The state or federal government is the author of the penalty, stating what it is and attending with rigid insistence to its execution.

But we say, "Scripture plainly tells us that the Devil 'has the power of death'" (Hebrews 2:14).

This means only that the Devil has the power to entice men into sin, the penalty for which, as prescribed by God, is death. B. F. Westcott states, "The Devil, as the author of sin, has the power over death, its consequence (Romans 5:12), *not as though he could inflict it at his pleasure; but death is his realm; he makes it subservient to his end.*"

The power of death belongs alone to God, and the Devil can have no part in it except as he receives his power from God. We may think of Satan as holding this dominion, but only as an executioner—never as a lord. The Devil has the power of death, not immediately, but mediately through sin, through which he delivers men over to God's judicial punishment of death.

Franz Delitzsch puts it well: "We cannot think of the Devil as the God-hating possessor of the power of death, without at the same time, since 'all things are for God and through God' (verse 10), thinking of his deadly power as subserving the will of God."

It becomes plain to any honest thinker or student of God's Word that only in a very limited or qualified sense can it be said that the Devil is the author of sickness, disease, and death. This limited and qualified power of the Devil is readily admitted, and this helps to explain passages such as the following:

> *Job 2:7:* Here we are told that "Satan . . . smote Job with sore boils from the sole of his foot unto his crown."
> *Luke 13:16:* Here we are told of a woman "whom Satan hath bound, lo, these many years."
> *Acts 10:38:* It is said here that Jesus healed "all that were oppressed of the devil."

Satan can work in this way *only* insofar as he gets permission from God. This seems to be clearly taught in the Book of Job.

Realizing that there was a wall around Job and his family and all Job's belongings, and that he could not touch Job in any way without God's permission, the Devil asked God's permission to afflict the faithful old saint to prove that he was hypocritically serving God for what he could get out of it.

The Almighty gave the Devil the permission he craved, but said, "Only upon himself put not forth thine hand." That is, "Don't touch Job himself."

The Devil destroyed Job's livestock, his buildings, and his children, but instead of cursing God, as the Devil said he would, Job praised Him.

Then the Devil asked permission to afflict the body of Job himself, and this too was granted by God, but with the restriction that Job's life must be spared.

Isn't this comforting? To know that the child of God is thus hedged about by the protecting love and power of the omnipotent God, and that Satan cannot touch the weakest saint to do him bodily harm without the permission of this God!

Yet we find ourselves asking, do we not, Wherein is the great difference between God's permissive will and His direct will?

If for any purpose God decides that a "thorn in the flesh," a siege of sickness, is needed in your experience or mine—whether He uses the office of Satan to bring it about, or causes it to be brought about in any other way—assuredly it would never be brought about at all except as the result of His will.

Generally speaking, our health is the will of God. But this does not mean that sometimes it is not best for a saint to suffer and that because of the divine knowledge of this fact, the chastening hand of God is to be seen in the affliction.

There also are many passages in the Bible that seem to indicate that God sees sickness directly as the expression of His own will.

Genesis 12:17 tells us that "*Jehovah plagued Pharaoh with great plagues*," meaning certain contagious diseases common in Egypt.

Exodus 9:1–12 says that it was through direct action of the Lord that the Egyptian cattle were diseased and ulcerous boils came upon the Egyptians themselves.

Exodus 15:26 states that Jehovah said, "*I will put* none of these diseases [plagues] upon thee, *which I have brought* upon the Egyptians."

Exodus 32:35 tells us that *the Lord sent disease* on the Israelites "because they made the calf, which Aaron made."

We are not without certain other Scriptures that seem to indicate that human pain is often the will of God.

First Peter 3:17 tells us, "It is better, *if the will of God be so,* that ye suffer for well-doing, than for evil-doing." First Peter 4:19 says, "Wherefore let them that *suffer according to the will of God* commit the keeping of their souls to him in well-doing, as unto a faithful Creator."

It is said that these verses and a few others like them in 1 Peter refer to persecution and not to sickness of any kind. This is true in the main reference, but even so, if it is ever the will of God that we suffer pain, why may it not be equally His will that pain be induced through the afflictions of our bodily organs?

What greater pain has ever been endured than that suffered by many of the saints of old who have been persecuted "according to the will of God"?

Think of the stones that stung Stephen to death. Think of the stripes that Paul endured, and the axe that chopped off his head. Think of the spikes that fastened Peter upside down on his cross. Think of the flames that licked up the blood of Savonarola! Think of those who were "slain with the sword" and "sawn asunder" (Hebrews 11:37). Think of those who were devoured by lions, starved to death, or frozen on the Alpine mountainsides, and of the countless host who suffered in persecution the most excruciating torture and the most agonizing pains ever conceived by the human mind.

Certainly, if pain comes occasionally according to the will of God, we may ask what good reason is there for denying that sickness sometimes comes in the same way.

If this were not true, how would it be possible for God to "chasten whom He loveth"?

First Peter 4:12 tells us of "the fiery trial which is to try you." The psalmist long ago said, "It is good for me that I have been afflicted; that I might learn thy statutes" (Psalm 119:71). Hebrews 12:7 states that it is for the purpose of chastening (for our improvement as sons) that we endure suffering and persecution. Hebrews 12:10 says that while our fathers according to the flesh "chastised us after their own pleasure," God chastises us "for our profit, that we might be partakers of His holiness."

What better illustrations of all this than the experiences of Job and of Paul? Job was said to be the "perfect and upright man," and Paul was the man of mountain-faith and of a devotion to Christ that led him to the martyr's block. If such as these were the recipients of God's chastisement through sickness and disease—that Job might "repent in dust and ashes" (Job 42:6) and Paul might not "be exalted above measure" (2 Corinthians 12:7)—are we to believe that saints of today are to be exempt from such chastisement because they have "met the conditions" and are therefore more saintly and perfect than these holy and mighty men of God to whom we have referred by way of illustration?

The Bible says that God "scourgeth every son whom he receiveth." It says, "Whom the Lord loveth he chasteneth." It says, "If ye be without chastisement, then are ye bastards and not sons."

No, the simple truth of the matter, as Dr. James H. Brookes has said, is that, "There is no assurance in the written Word that our Father wills all His children to be exempt from sickness during this Dispensation of suffering, or that it would be best for them to be thus exempt. Nor is there a single promise, nor one line, from the first verse of Genesis to the last of Revelation, that pledges God to grant His power in response to prayer in every case of sickness, in little or in great attacks."

Hundreds of God's children have prayed for the healing of the sick, and God, in answer to their prayers, has graciously brought the afflicted one back to health. But hundreds more have called upon God in similar circumstances, and healing has not come. These were Christians just as earnest, consecrated, and devoted as those whose prayers were answered according to their desires.

Do you not think that Paul prayed for Trophimus, for Timothy, for Epaphroditus?

Yes, Christians have prayed, and prayer was made as in the Word of God we have been told to pray. They have agreed together (Matthew 18:19), have made full confession of sin (James 5:15–16), have separated themselves from every known form of sin (Psalm 66:18), have agonized in prayer (Acts 12:5), prayed in His name, as they earnestly believed (John 14:13), prayed the prayer of faith (James 5:14).

Yes, they have prayed for others and no healing has come, because healing in these particular instances was apparently not the will of God. They have prayed for themselves, even as Paul did, and received only the assurance from the throne of heaven that the sufficient grace of God for enduring the suffering was something much better than the coveted relief from it could possibly be.

Surely, with the Word of God speaking in the plainest and most indisputable way, and in the face of the experience of many of God's choicest saints and mightiest men of faith, as recorded both in His Word and on the pages of history since—surely it is unwarranted presumption to say that it is *always*, in each and every particular instance, the will of God to heal the sick. To say that failure to receive healing is because the petitioners have not "met the conditions," or are living out of communion with God in some way, is not only anti-scriptural, but also a vicious dogmatic assertion of which our healing brethren ought not to be guilty.

We read of One—none other than the blessed Son of God Himself—who "learned . . . obedience by the things which he suffered" (Hebrews 5:8), who "himself also was *compassed with infirmity*" (Hebrews 5:2), who was made "perfect through sufferings" (Hebrews 2:10), and "in that he himself hath suffered being tempted, he is able to succour them that are tempted" (Hebrews 2:18).

Jesus' sacrificial sufferings are largely in view in these verses, but it is clear that these sufferings are not to be confined to His death alone. He suffered all along the way to the cross. There are those who would have us believe that inasmuch as "he was touched with the *feeling* of our infirmities," He must have suffered much in the same way we have been called upon to suffer.

Nevertheless, if He "learned obedience" and was made "perfect through suffering" of any kind, certainly we, who are His followers, are not so rich in grace that we have need of nothing that we can learn through suffering.

Part II

The Practice of Prayer

CHAPTER 11

The Prayers of Paul

The apostle Paul was the great prayer warrior of the New Testament. In studying his prayers we note that his burden was for spiritual power rather than for temporal power. Throughout the epistles many illustrations of this can be found.

1. His Prayer for Pentecost: "That Christ may dwell in your hearts by faith; that ye, being rooted and grounded in love, may be able to comprehend with all saints what is the breadth, and length, and depth, and height; and to know the love of Christ, which passeth knowledge, that ye might be filled with all the fulness of God" (Ephesians 3:17–19).

2. His Prayer for Perception: "For this cause we also, since the day we heard it, do not cease to pray for you, and to desire that ye might be filled with the knowledge of his will in all wisdom and spiritual understanding; that ye might walk worthy of the Lord unto all pleasing, being fruitful in every good work, and increasing in the knowledge of God" (Colossians 1:9–10).

3. *His Prayer for Purity:* "And the very God of peace sanctify you wholly; and I pray God your whole spirit and soul and body be preserved blameless unto the coming of our Lord Jesus Christ. Faithful is he that calleth you, who also will do it" (1 Thessalonians 5:23–24).

4. *His Prayer for Power:* "Wherefore I also, after I heard of your faith in the Lord Jesus, and love unto all the saints, cease not to give thanks for you, making mention of you in my prayers; that the God of our Lord Jesus Christ, the Father of glory, may give unto you the spirit of wisdom and revelation in the knowledge of him: the eyes of your understanding being enlightened; that ye may know what is the hope of his calling, and what the riches of the glory of his inheritance in the saints, and what is the exceeding greatness of his power to us-ward who believe, according to the working of his mighty power, which he wrought in Christ, when he raised him from the dead, and set him at his own right hand in the heavenly places" (Ephesians 1:15–20).

5. *His Prayer for Perseverance:* "And this I pray, that your love may abound yet more and more in knowledge and in all judgment; that ye may approve things that are excellent; that ye may be sincere and without offence till the day of Christ; being filled with the fruits of righteousness, which are by Jesus Christ, unto the glory and praise of God" (Philippians 1:9–11).

6. *His Prayer for Perfectness:* "Now the God of peace, that brought again from the dead our Lord Jesus, that great shepherd of the sheep, through the blood of the everlasting covenant, make you perfect in every good work to do his will, working in you that which is well-pleasing in his sight, through Jesus Christ; to whom be glory for ever and ever. Amen" (Hebrews 13:20–21).

7. *His Prayer for Peace:* "Now the Lord of peace himself give you peace always by all means. The Lord be with you all" (2 Thessalonians 3:16).

In subsequent chapters we will study some of Paul's classic prayers. But the most exciting and immediate demonstration of the effectiveness of Paul's praying can be found in the famed account of the Philippian jailer (Acts 16:16ff.).

Paul and Silas had been preaching the gospel in the city of Philippi. Many people were listening to them and accepting Jesus Christ as their Savior from sin. One woman, possessed with the spirit of divination, met the apostles and followed them for several days. She cried, "These men are the servants of the most high God, which shew unto us the way of salvation."

Paul recognized the spirit as an evil one and was grieved. He said to the spirit, "I command thee in the name of Jesus Christ to come out of her." He came out of her, but when this woman's masters saw what had happened and saw that their hope of material gain was gone, they became angry with Paul and Silas. The masters brought them to the rulers and before long succeeded in having Paul and Silas beaten. When these men of God had suffered many stripes, and no doubt were torn and bleeding, they were thrown into prison.

The jailer was given strict orders to keep them secure. Fearing that Paul and Silas might in some miraculous way escape from prison, the jailer cast them into the inner prison. It was well known that apostles in times past had escaped prison doors. God had repeatedly released them from prison to continue proclaiming the gospel (Acts 5:19; 12:7–10). But there in the inner prison, facing the prospect of death, Paul and Silas prayed at midnight.

Paul's prayer was powerful in its effect. The other prisoners heard their songs of praise and loud prayers.

Then came the earthquake. We may be sure that Paul and Silas were quite calm and expectant when the foundations of the prison were shaken. But the jailer was frantic. He knew he had been given orders that Paul and Silas especially should be watched over carefully and kept safely.

With open doors caused by the earthquake, the prisoners free to escape, the jailer felt that he would rather take his own life than face the authorities. Paul knew, however, that had the jailer taken his own life, it would have been much worse for him to face God in the hereafter than to face the authorities now. Paul was quick to take control of the situation, and probably encouraged the prisoners to remain in the prison, even though the doors were open. When the jailer drew out his sword to kill himself, Paul cried with a loud voice, "Do thyself no harm: for we are all here."

Note that it was not Paul and Silas's praying and singing that awoke the jailer. God was so moved by the praying and singing that He sent an earthquake, and *then* the jailer awoke. What powerful praying, that the jailer's heart should be smitten as he trembled in the inky blackness of a damaged prison! It was too dark to find his way to Paul and Silas, but when a light was provided for him, he sprang to the two apostles and fell down before them. In sincere repentance he cried out, "What must I do to be saved?" With hearts filled with joy, they answered, "Believe on the Lord Jesus Christ, and thou shalt be saved, and thy house." Then for a long time Paul and Silas spoke to the jailer and explained in detail the way of salvation and the Word of the Lord. Not only was the jailer himself born again that night, but all his household.

What a reward for a short time of praise and prayer! Does God move hearts when we pray? Indeed, He does! When someone laughs at us for being Christians, do we feel ashamed and pity ourselves that someone said something? Or, maybe, as we are in the service of the Lord, the trials are many as we give ourselves completely to His work. When we receive opposition or ridicule, are we ready to throw up our hands and say, "I'm through"?

When things are the hardest, it is the time to pray and sing praises to God. *Too often we give up just before God intended to send an earthquake.* God might not send an earthquake during the first five minutes we pray. It might not come until midnight, in the hardest hours of our lives, when things look the most hopeless. Be encouraged to press on, powerful in prayer, until the jailer and his household whom God has placed in our pathways hear the gospel message from our lips and have turned to the Lord with their whole hearts.

CHAPTER 12

How to Pray
Your First Prayer

(Paul's Prayer of Commitment)

Paul was a man of prayer. His writings are replete with experiences of prayer, teachings on prayer, and the results of prayer.

As we study the writings of Paul we find the rich vein of a deep prayer life. Our faith is increased by Paul's steel-like hope, revealed in what he asked of the Father. Paul's eloquence and unshakable faith in prayer speaks volumes of his personal communication with God.

The first prayer of Paul—then named Saul—is found in Acts 9:6. When he prayed this prayer, he was not saved. After he prayed, he was!

This two-sentence prayer was the simplest one Paul ever prayed, but it brought about his new birth. It was his conversion prayer; it changed his name from Saul to Paul; it changed his life. He was no longer the instrument of destruction toward the church, for now he knew he was God's chosen vessel. This short prayer gave birth to the regeneration of a mind and a spirit who became the vehicle that brought us the theology of the Christian church. Paul was ready to be the instrument for the authorship of more than half the New Testament.

This simple first prayer shook the first century, and its result continues to shake the world.

Before Saul prayed, he was prayed *for* by the dying deacon, Stephen. As Stephen was being stoned to death by a mob, Saul looked on and consented to his murder (Acts 7:57–8:1).

Saul was a man of prominence, authority, and power. He was greatly feared. He went before the Sanhedrin and demanded authority over the Christians, and it was quickly granted. He was a persuasive and brilliant man, having been educated at the feet of Gamaliel, one of the most honored teachers Judaism ever produced.

Saul himself had become a leader of the Pharisees . . . "a Pharisee of the Pharisees." Now, as a ruler, he taught others. His teaching in the New Testament letters undoubtedly shows that he was one of the most brilliant men who ever lived. But he never exercised his great potential and capacity more than on the day he first prayed to the Lord. Until then, despite his intellectual and religious powers, Saul was a fanatic against Christ.

> And Saul, yet breathing out threatenings and slaugh-
> ter against the disciples of the Lord. *Acts 9:1*

The expression "yet" indicates Paul worked ceaselessly. "Breathing out" means everywhere he went there was an atmosphere of antagonism, of evil, of judgment, of persecution, and of death. Being religious in his fanaticism, he went right to the high priest, the chief leader of the Jews, and requested certain official documents, "letters to Damascus to the synagogues" asserting authority to make house arrests against those of "this way."

Before the faith came to be called Christianity, it was called "the way," because of Jesus' statement, "I am the Way" (John 14:6). Saul wanted to bring anyone who was following "the way," professing faith in Christ, "whether they were men or women," bound to Jerusalem, the religious center of Judaism. The expression "whether men or women" was significant, because women traditionally were never subject to religious persecution. In his zeal Paul threw away all the decent rules of the day. His zeal boiled over to block out reason. Yet he was prayed for by Stephen. Stephen's dying words were a prayer of forgiveness that applied to Paul as well as to the rest of his persecutors: "Lord, lay not this sin to their charge" (Acts 7:60). Before Paul prayed, he was prayed for. "The effectual fervent prayer of a righteous man availeth much" (James 5:16).

God stopped Saul. He stopped Saul so he would pray. God was honoring Stephen's prayer (Acts 9:3): "And as he journeyed . . ."

This shows us when God speaks—in the everyday course of our lives. He speaks right where we are. "He came near Damascus: and suddenly there shined round about him a light from heaven: and he fell to the earth and heard a voice saying, Saul, Saul, why persecutest thou me?" (vv. 3–4).

God stopped Saul and was the only one who would have done so. On the ground the powerful, hell-bent sinner heard his name twice, Saul, Saul. Why twice? Perhaps it was God's double calling to salvation and service.

Here Saul really prayed for the first time in his life. He prayed to the living Lord, but it was not in a way he ever dreamed he would pray. Here was a man of prominence, of brilliance, of authority, of power, and of religious dignity, humbled in the dust of Damascus. He was no longer breathing out threats, no longer breathing out slaughter, no longer breathing out fear.

Humbly, meekly, trembling he cried, "Who art thou, Lord?" (v. 5). "What wilt thou have me do?" (v. 6). Saul's first prayer asked two simple questions: who and what? It was a great prayer. It was personal. It was direct. It came from the heart.

God answered that prayer of a confused man, without

delay. When we go before Him on our knees, God is ready to listen. Two little questions, yet they contain all the ingredients that are essential to prayer. Everything else is derived from that. Once you have settled these two questions, you've got it all.

"Lord, who are you?" Confession, worship, and praise all come naturally when we settle in our minds the centrality of the truth, "Who is Jesus Christ?" When He is Lord, He gets my money, my allegiance, my home, my mind, my body, my soul, my will, my worship, my praise, my adoration, and my desires—my everything. All flow naturally from a knowing heart.

True prayer brought for Saul, and brings for us, a real sense of the presence of God. There is no question that God was there. Saul perceived a light, heard a voice, and responded, "Lord, who are you?" By the Spirit we sense the presence of God; by His Word we hear the voice of God and can know that we are before Him and thus respond, "Lord." Real prayer makes us know that we are in the presence of God.

"Lord, what will you have me do?" If we are honest, we must admit that most of our prayers are *telling* God what to do. "God, bless this service. Take care of my family. Give me good health." We almost come to the point of saying, "Lord, here are Your orders for the day."

But it must be the other way around. It has to be Private Bisagno reporting before General Jesus, saying, "What will *You* have *Me* to do?" Our prayers need a whole lot more listening and openness, rather than requesting and demanding of God.

In one way, this was not the first prayer Saul ever prayed. He was a religious leader among the Jews, a Pharisee of the stock of Benjamin. He had all the credentials. He knew what it meant to recite his prayers. He knew what it meant to memorize his prayers. He knew what it meant to stand in front of the mirror and practice his prayers. The Pharisees did this repeatedly. So Saul was a man of prayer. He knew prayer. He understood prayer. He read volumes on it.

But this was probably his first prayer that ever got through to heaven. No matter who we are—preacher, rabbi, priest, millionaire, pauper, up and out, down and out—God is not obligated to answer our prayers until we first pray the sinner's prayer: "God, be merciful to me, a sinner." First we must be converted, born again. We must deal with our sins. We must become children of God before we can be assured He answers us.

Now, you may say, "But I have prayed, and God answered me before I was saved." Perhaps someone else was praying. Remember, Stephen prayed for Saul. Perhaps someone else was praying for your sick child or for your prosperity. Perhaps we will be surprised when the heavenly rewards are given out to find that the people who stood before great crowds and preached with world-wide fame are standing in the back of the line. At the front of the line may be a little unknown widow lady from the hills of West Virginia who was *praying* for that preacher. God might be answering someone else's prayer, or it may be that God was going to let that event happen anyway to get your attention. Perhaps your prayer just coincided with what God had already planned.

The point is, God doesn't have to answer your prayers. He is not obligated to answer the prayers of the unbeliever, nor even to hear them. This self-sufficient, arrogant, educated, proud man named Saul, all wrapped up in himself, probably prayed his first prayer that ever really got through to God that day on the way to Damascus.

It is noteworthy that it was the Lord Himself who initiated the prompting to prayer. Saul wasn't thinking about either God or prayer. God dramatically burst into the affairs of his life and did something so fantastic that he couldn't do anything else *but* pray. We may well say that most of the motivations and the impressions of the Holy Spirit to pray are not nearly so dramatic as Saul's, but they're just as *real*. I learned a long time ago that sometimes in a worship service, sometimes driving down the road, sometimes in study, when I feel deeply the impress of the Spirit of God to pray, I need to just stop everything and say, "Let's pray."

I was at a statewide convention in Oklahoma twenty years ago. The brethren were debating an issue when one pious soul got up and said, "Mr. Chairman, I make a motion that we stop and pray." The chairman wisely said, "Brother, we don't have to have a motion to pray, let's just pray." Indeed, we don't have to have a motion. We don't even have to have the prompting of the Spirit. "Men ought always to pray, and not to faint" (Luke 18:1). But it is imperative that when we *do* feel the gentle prompting of the Spirit to pray, that we, like Saul, *do* pray!

Saul's prayer began as an act of contrition before God. "And he fell to the earth" (Acts 9:4). Even if we do not say a word aloud or move a muscle, prayer is first of all properly positioning ourselves before the Lord. Saul was not ready to see and know who God is until he first got himself in the right position. For Saul, at that time, the right position was flat on his face.

This does not mean that we must always raise our hands or never raise our hands. Or that we must always stand or never stand. It does not mean that we always have to pray kneeling. We can pray standing, or with heads raised rather than bowed. But this verse means that the posture of the heart must be lifted up to God. The posture of contrition is the soul kneeling before God; and God in return is being exalted above man. The true posture of prayer is humility before an exalted God. It is not the position of the body, but the posture of the heart that gets the prayer through.

God listens to us because He knows all about us. Knowing all about us, He knows precisely what we need and has something specific and personal to say to us.

Did the Lord know anything about Saul of Tarsus? Of

course. First, He knew his name—"Saul." Second, He knew what he was doing—"Why persecutest thou me?" Saul didn't lay a hand on Jesus directly, but he did so indirectly by persecuting His people. When we touch God's people, we touch God. God knew more about what Saul was doing than Paul did himself.

How many foolish mistakes do we make because we do not take the Lord into account and ask for His direction? We think we are doing the right thing, while exactly the opposite may be true. God knew how Saul felt. "Saul, it is hard to kick against the cattle goad, isn't it? This prodding, this guilt, this troubling of the Spirit are hard to live with, aren't they? You're fighting me, you're going against me" (see Acts 9:5). There is no other suggestion in the Bible that Paul was feeling miserable in his soul about what he was doing, but God knew.

Can we afford to open up our brains, our subconsciouses, our motives, our instincts, our minds, our hearts, the totality of our being to One who knows all about us? Only if that Someone loves us with a *love equal to His knowledge*. It is important to note that God wanted to speak to Saul, and wants to speak to us, because He knows what is needed and He wants to help.

Before Saul prayed, he was haughty, proud, and self-sufficient. He was breathing out slaughter "against the disciples of the Lord." He was against Christians, and he was against Christ. He was the "darling" of the religious establishment. But after he prayed, Saul was broken, humble, and kneeling before the Lord. He was *for* Christ and Christians. Immediately he was preaching Christ. He was risking his life for Christ. He became hunted by the establishment.

Did prayer change anything? Like all real prayer, it changed everything.

CHAPTER 13

How to Pray for Those We Love

(Paul's Prayer for the Colossians)

For this cause we also, since the day we heard it, do not cease to pray for you, and to desire that ye might be filled with the knowledge of his will in all wisdom and spiritual understanding; That ye might walk worthy of the Lord unto all pleasing, being fruitful in every good work, and increasing in the knowledge of God; Strengthened with all might, according to his glorious power, unto all patience and longsuffering with joyfulness. *Colossians 1:9–11*

This prayer is beautiful and warm. The apostle Paul is opening his heart and pouring out his love. In this experience he shows us how to pray for those for whom we care very much.

Paul prayed this unselfish prayer, completely other-centered, from a heart bursting with love for his spiritual children under the most severe and drastic of circumstances. He was in prison in Rome.

I have visited the Mamertine prison, where Paul was kept. One has to climb down a ladder into a cell about ten feet deep and about as large as a small church choir loft. The prison is damp and dirty. The room, walls, and floor have literally been carved out of granite. The only way into it is from the top, for there are no doors or windows.

Here lived a man who was hated by the Roman Empire and cursed by his Roman guards because he preached allegiance to Jesus Christ. To the point of death, he refused to worship Nero and call him "Lord." So in that prison hole they spat on him, cursed him, and chained him between two guards.

Everything Paul wrote, for this and other reasons, he dictated to somebody else to write—too weak to hold a pen, too blind to see to write, or too sick. But he was not physically incapable of praying for those whom he loved.

We expect people who are free to pray for people who are in jail. We expect healthy people to pray for sick people. The people who have means should care and pray for the poor. But Paul gives us an example of the very essence of Christianity—that people pray for people not only *less* fortunate, but *more* fortunate than they.

It is unusual for those who are poor to pray, "God, bless the rich." It is strange to hear the sick and dying pray for those who are well. But often, when I sit by the bedside of a seriously ill member, I hear, "Pastor, I've been praying for you."

I rejoice that in Africa and South America, people in jungles, grass huts, and poverty pray, "O God, bless American Christians. Bless our brothers in America who have sent Brother Bisagno over here. Bless his church, and bless his family." They seemingly pray more earnestly for us than we do for them.

Blessed are the poor who pray for the rich.

Blessed are the sick who pray for the well.

Paul was praying for the people at Colosse under great difficulty and adversity.

Furthermore, he was praying for people he had never seen, yet loved. As far as we know, Paul never went to

Colosse. Somebody else had been there first and started the work, one of his spiritual children. So he was writing to his spiritual grandchildren.

"Since we heard of your faith in Christ Jesus" (Colossians 1:4). He had only heard of their testimony. He didn't know them personally.

"As ye also learned of Epaphras . . ." (1:7): Epaphras had been there and started the church. He won the converts. He baptized the new people. He got it started, not Paul. "Who also declared unto us your love in the spirit" (1:8). All Paul knew was what Epaphras had told him about the church at Colosse. "For this cause we also, since the day we *heard* it . . ." (1:9). Paul makes it clear that he was praying for people he had never seen.

If we are inspired by example and exhorted by Scripture to pray for fellow believers whom we have never seen, how much more ought we daily to pray for our loved ones whom we have seen.

Paul prayed that they might, first, *receive* something; in order that they might, second, *do* something; so that they may, third, *be* something. "For this cause we also, since the day we heard it, do not cease to pray for you, and to desire that ye might be filled with the knowledge of his will in all wisdom and spiritual understanding" (1:9).

1. *Paul prayed for his loved ones to have a certain kind of mindset, a certain kind of attitude.* "Desire that ye might be filled with the knowledge of his will" (1:9). The most important thing in the world for them to know was the will of God. They couldn't do what they didn't know. Let us pray every day for our loved ones and for our friends that they will receive the knowledge of His will. I can tell you a hundred ways God shows us His will: by circumstance, by the "holy hunch," by the inner voice of His Spirit, by the Word of God. But we must first be willing to do His will.

Knowing the will of God has a great deal to do with desire. We must desire to receive God's knowledge of His will. The attitude of many people is, "My mind is made up—don't confuse me with the facts." A woman once said to me, "Pray for my son. He's praying that the Lord will show him what He wants him to do, so he can see whether it's something he wants to do or not." That doesn't work. One must desire to receive, "Thy will be done. . . ."

The knowledge of God's will comes from reading His Word. The Scripture conditions our hearts to know the will of God. We may not find His will directly in a particular passage, but the Word will put us in an attitude to receive it.

If we are open, honest, and sincere, God will place the desire to do His will in our hearts. The first thing we should pray is that God will reveal the knowledge of His will to those whom we love.

Paul added something extra for his loved ones—"and spiritual understanding." This phrase means two things. It means a discerning spirit, a certain perceptiveness about people and life that the Holy Spirit gives. It also means insight into the Scriptures. This causes us to grow in relating the Word of God to everyday life. Therefore we should pray that our loved ones will have a mindset of spiritual understanding of the will of God.

2. *We should pray that our loved ones will do something with God's will.* The will of God is intended to show us how to live. God's will is to be translated into practical, everyday terms that make a difference in the way we live. Paul says, ". . . that ye might walk worthy of the Lord" (Colossians 1:10).

"Walking worthy" means the way we live. Does this mean we can live so as to be worthy of salvation? No, but we can be worthy of the name of the Lord who has given us our salvation. It means that we can live in such a way that we will be an honor to Jesus Christ and not a discredit to Him. In this way we can rightfully be called Christians, and people won't be surprised to find out that we are.

116

"Ye might walk worthy of the Lord unto all pleasing" (v. 10). What happens when a person pleases the Lord and walks in such a manner as to be worthy of the name Christian? He becomes fruitful in everything he does. He is spiritually prosperous. If he is an athlete, then every team member knows he is a Christian, and usually someone on that team becomes a Christian. Every girl he continues to date will probably become a Christian. In every business relationship his partners will know Christ is first in his life. "In every good work" (v. 10), in everything he does, he is bearing fruit and productive and making a spiritual difference.

"And increasing in the knowledge of God" (v. 10). The result of a person who pleases God, bearing fruit in every good work, is this: God will in turn complete the cycle and give him more knowledge that he may grow all the more. Jesus said, "You have been faithful over little, I'll make you ruler over much" (see Matthew 25:23). The more faithful we are with the knowledge of the will of God, the more He gives us.

3. *We should pray for strength for our loved ones.* The strength we are asking is His power, the power of the indwelling Spirit who gives the ability to discern His will, to have wisdom, to live right, to please Him, to bear fruit, and to receive more knowledge. All this comes from the Holy Spirit, who gives us strength.

Our loved ones need this strength from the Lord, the end result being "patience and longsuffering with joy-fulness" (Colossians 1:11). Do you realize how many times the Scripture admonishes us to rejoice in the middle of trouble, sickness, divorce, depression, or failure? This strength is given that we can go right through these problems with fullness of joy in Christ. Through it all, we can rejoice in Jesus and praise the Lord anyhow.

Almost every book of the Bible teaches us about trials. What is a trial? It is a mess we can't get out of. It is a difficulty with no solution. If our income tax comes due or the roof leaks or some other urgent need arises and we need $14,000, it isn't a trial if we are able to get a loan from our banker. But if the banker says, "I wouldn't loan you fifty bucks," we have a trial. Then we are in a heap of trouble! A trial is something we can't get out of, but have to suffer through.

Praying that our loved ones get through a trial is not really enough. While they are going through the "fire," they need God's strength of "patience" and "longsuffering" that will end the trial with "joyfulness." Without this strength, we are tempted in the middle of the trial to curse God, demanding, "Why did you get me into this?" Some quit going to church, backslide, and say, "What's the use?" and start living for the Devil. Pray that your loved ones will keep on rejoicing in Jesus. Pray that their trial will be met with strength, patience, and longsuffering. Pray that they will "praise the Lord anyhow."

I love Job. When everything in his world was crumbling around him, his wife began to chide him: "Husband, look what's happening to you! Just go ahead and sin! Renounce your faith! Curse God and let Him kill you and die." I like Job's answer to his distraught wife: "Mrs. Job, let me tell you something. I don't care if He does kill me! I'll go to my grave praising Him. Though He slay me, yet will I trust Him."

That's the kind of faith in the Lord we need to pray that our loved ones may have. This prayer by Paul is a complete prayer to pray over the ones we love. It asks that they receive the knowledge to know the will of God for themselves; then upon receiving it, that they will do the will of the Lord. Then it asks that they continue in the strength of His might.

Every parent ought to memorize this prayer and bless their children with it. It's the kind of prayer to pray over our children *every* day. Pray it in their hearing, and pray it regularly. It's a prayer that fits every home, every family, every loved one.

CHAPTER 14

How to Pray for the Here and Now

(Paul's Prayer for the Ephesians)

Wherefore I also, after I heard of your faith in the Lord Jesus, and love unto all the saints, Cease not to give thanks for you, making mention of you in my prayers; That the God of our Lord Jesus Christ, the Father of glory, may give unto you the spirit of wisdom and revelation in the knowledge of him: The eyes of your understanding being enlightened; that ye may know what is the hope of his calling, and what the riches of the glory of his inheritance in the saints, And what is the exceeding greatness of his power to us-ward who believe, according to the working of his mighty power. (*Ephesians* 1:15–19)

Paul encapsulates three important ingredients in his prayer for the here and now: hope, riches, and power. This prayer for the Ephesian believers is for them to receive the knowledge of "the hope of His calling, the riches of His glory, and the greatness of His power."

Paul makes a practical application in augmenting his prayer ingredients. It was for the Ephesians' enlightenment in the present. He prayed, "That you may specifically receive the spirit of wisdom and revelation in the knowledge of Him."

Paul's desire is that through this spiritual understanding they may live life at its best. That means that their eyes will be opened to the hope, riches, and power that belong to them as God's children.

1. *The first thing Paul prays is for understanding the hope of their calling as Christians.* Understanding His will makes a difference in how we live. Knowing His will affects our thinking, and our thinking affects our living. "As [a man] thinketh in his heart, so is he" (Proverbs 23:7).

The *hope* of the believer is to be contrasted with the *hopelessness* of the unbeliever. Hope in Jesus Christ is contrasted with hope outside Him. Bible hope is different from secular hope. "The hope of your calling" has everything to do with the God-oriented life. "Hope" expresses the sum total of the Christian faith. It is God-centered, and all of life moves from that focal point. The God-oriented person centers all his life around all that is hope.

It makes a difference what kind of hope we have. Hope in God through Christ, or hope in the world through humanism. Hope in the promises of God, or hope in the logic of man. Hope in creation by God, or hope in creation by accident. Hope in facts by God's Word, or hope in the theory of evolution.

The world's view of hope is, in fact, absolute hopelessness because it is lived without Him who is ultimate hope. It lives a meaningless, godless, secular existence. Humanism has no god, no purpose, and consequently no hope.

The secular hope of the unbeliever is little more than a "shot in the dark." A kind of fatalistic "lots of luck" or "I'll take my chances" or "hope against hope" or "well, I hope so." There is nothing tangible or real about the secular meaning of hope. It is little more than a fingers-crossed chance that maybe everything will work out okay.

To the Christian, hope is the opposite. There is a

futuristic overtone to the expression "the hope of the believer." It is a movement toward a consummation of all things for good under a sovereign God. That means everything we believe in is going somewhere and that somehow, in Jesus Christ, it all works out to victory for us.

Hope is not a blind alley for the believer. The hope of our calling that Paul prays about is an ultimate reality toward which we know the essence of the Christian faith is moving. Therefore, hope in the biblical sense or christological sense moves toward the ultimate lordship of Jesus Christ over all things. It has strong overtones that refer to the end of the world and the second coming of Christ.

So Bible hope has in view not a fatalistic shot in the dark, but a confidence that we know everything in the earth, in the body, in all the universe is moving toward a glorified, perfect state of union under the control of and in fellowship with the Lord Jesus Christ. It embodies all that we are and believe as Christians, primarily as it relates to the ultimate victory of Christ over everything.

When we talk about hope, we don't mean "lots of luck." We mean the embodiment of everything the gospel promises, declares, and provides.

Paul used the word *hope* as if it had already taken place. You and I wonder, "How can we sin and still get to heaven? How can we keep from losing our salvation? How do we keep from bailing out somewhere along the way?" Salvation in the Bible, from God's perspective, is not viewed from street level. We see a parade go by piece by piece. "Well, there's a float and here's a band and down the street rides a cowboy on a horse." But God has a better view. He doesn't have to wait to see the individual events as they go by. If we stand on a tall building and look down, we can see the beginning and ending of the parade all at once. We view the whole thing in perspective.

Our hope is assured in heaven because of what God had already planned to do before the creation of the world. He chose us. What He provided on the cross in dying for us, what He is doing in sanctifying us now, guarantees what He will do in the future.

The assurance, the guarantee of the accomplishment of our hope is predicated on what God has already done for us. It's not up for grabs whether we make it or not, or hang on faithfully or not. We don't have to guess and wonder whether what He has promised us will become a reality. It will be. It is promised. It is assured. And the assurance is based upon what He has already done. So what God planned to do from the foundation of the world, what Jesus Christ is doing now and will eternally do at the right hand of the Father, covers the extremities of the beginning and the end of our lives.

We must have a good grasp of all that is offered to us in our calling as followers of Jesus Christ.

2. *The second thing Paul prays about is our possession. God wants us to have a knowledge of the riches of the glory of His inheritance.* This is important, because Paul said, "My God shall supply all your need according to his riches in glory by Christ Jesus" (Philippians 4:19). This sounds as if Paul's talking about physical sustenance. But he is speaking of what is ours in the riches of the glory of his inheritance, not in heaven, but in the saints. The expression "in the saints" in Ephesians 1:18 indicates a locative sphere where the riches of His glory operates. All that there is in the hope of his calling and the consummate victory under Jesus Christ is wonderful, but Paul pulls us right back to earth and says in essence, "But don't be so preoccupied with it that you miss its earthly value." The expression "in the saints" (not in heaven) is very important. The inheritance is in God's people.

Paul writes that the riches of God's glory lie in the greatest earthly treasure of all, in the saints. God's people are more important than the hope toward which they are moving. God's people, His presence in His people, and fellowship with the people are more important to God than what He has prepared for them. Fellowship with God *now* is more important than the rewards of God *later on.*

So Paul says, "I want you to understand the riches of the glory of his inheritance," not in heaven, but in the saints right here and now.

There are three senses in which the glory of God is in the saints. First, God *will glorify* His saints. We are moving toward a union with Him in which He will have glorified His saints. Second, He is daily being glorified *by* His saints. Every time we come together and praise Him, every time we serve Him, we are glorifying Him. He is going to glorify His saints. He is being glorified by His saints. And third, God says our priority now is that He be glorified *in* His saints. He's talking about the priority of the fellowship of a New Testament church. In His high priestly prayer Jesus said, "Father, I pray that they all might be one, that the world might know I came from you" (see John 17:21).

A church can do without buildings, but it can't get along without harmony in the fellowship. It is in the unity of the body that God reveals His glory in His saints. One day He will glorify His saints, but until this hope of our calling in the future starts, He is blessing and benefiting the world through the riches of His inheritance by glorifying Himself now in His people.

"It's wonderful," Paul says, "to talk about the sweet by-and-by, but don't get so taken up with what is yours in the hope of your calling that you forget the riches of your inheritance right now." And how are His glory and His riches to be lived out in the world? In His body, the fellowship of the saints.

3. *We have looked at the promise of what's ours in the future and the possession that's ours now.* The third ingredient in Paul's prayer for the here and now is the power to live out this beautiful concept.

Paul prays, "And what is the exceeding greatness of His power to us-ward who believe." It all happens by the power of God, and nothing must be allowed to stop the power. No divisiveness in the fellowship, no doctrinal error, no evil, no rebellion. Nothing! The body must be in harmony with itself and with the Lord.

What kind of power produces the fellowship? In verse 20 Paul tells us it is the resurrection power, "which He wrought in Christ when He raised him from the dead and set him at his own right hand in the heavenly places." God made a dramatic demonstration of His power and brought His only begotten Son back to life. "Now the God who did that," Paul says, "has that same power inside of you to build harmony in the fellowship, perpetuating the presence of God in the saints." On top of that, there's glory in the future in the hope of His calling and all that it is moving toward. It's all possible because of the power of God. We should understand that and rejoice in that. God is in His people. The power of God sustains us here and now and is our hope till we all get to heaven.

If we get a good grasp on understanding the hope of our calling, of the riches of the glory of our inheritance, and the exceeding greatness of the power of God, we will surely wear the crown of life.

CHAPTER 15

How to Pray for the Spiritually Sick

(Paul's Prayer for the Corinthians)

I thank my God always on your behalf, for the grace of God which is given you by Jesus Christ; That in every thing ye are enriched by him, in all utterance, and in all knowledge; Even as the testimony of Christ was confirmed in you: So that ye come behind in no gift; waiting for the coming of our Lord Jesus Christ: Who shall also confirm you unto the end, that ye may be blameless in the day of our Lord Jesus Christ. God is faithful, by whom ye were called unto the fellowship of his Son Jesus Christ our Lord. (1 Corinthians 1:4–9)

Paul's prayer for the spiritually sick Corinthian church was more experiential than academic.

The Corinthian letter is a study in spiritual surgery. Like a good physician, Paul prepares his patient for surgery with a good anesthetic. The anesthetic Paul uses lets them know at the outset that in spite of their anxiety for the operation, he is concerned for their comfort.

Paul prepares his readers for spiritual surgery by assuring them that the security of their life in Christ was their ultimate comfort and hope. In this short prayer of six verses Paul refers to Jesus five times. He wants them to understand positionally who and what they are in Christ so that they can move toward becoming experientially what they are both positionally and potentially. He tells them six things for which he thanks God about them so that they will understand the divine surgery is remedial and redemptive.

These six great truths will help a person with any kind of spiritual sickness begin to get well.

1. *"I thank God for the grace of God which is given you by Jesus Christ."* Paul first thanks God for their standing in grace. The word "grace" simply means something we have but don't deserve. I do not merit or earn or deserve anything I have. It is all given to me on the basis of Jesus' merits and worth and what He has imparted to me. That's grace. Paul wants his readers to understand all they are is because of Jesus Christ.

What is the problem of evil? It is the problem of pride, rebellion, and independence from God. The first step toward solving the problem is a reemphasis of our standing, not in independence from, but in union with Jesus Christ. We will never change our course of action until we come to appreciate who we are, accepted and beloved children of God. The Corinthians' standing in grace, then, is essential to the first step in motivating them to get spiritually well.

In verse 4, "For the grace of God which is given you *by Jesus Christ*" should be translated, *"in Jesus Christ."* Everything we are is because we are in Him. Everything we possess is because we are in Him. Everything we may become, experience, and enjoy is because we are "in Jesus Christ." The very breath in our body, our right to exist, is because He is our Creator. Our salvation, the family of God, the Word of God, the Holy Spirit, the church, the joy, the fellowship, the promise, the comfort, the assurance, the coming, the home, the kingdom—everything we have is because of what we are *in* Jesus Christ. We must come to appreciate our standing in grace.

Let us observe four problems the Corinthians encountered due to an inadequate understanding of their standing in grace. For one thing, they obviously had their eyes off Jesus and on man. An incisive passage of Scripture begins in 1 Corinthians 1:11. "It hath been declared unto me"—somebody has told me about you—"my brethren, by them which are of the house of Chloe, that there are contentions among you." Can you imagine a body being divided? The foot saying, "I don't like the eye." The left ear saying, "I'm more important than the right ear." The whole church was split.

What were they split over? "Now this I say, that every one of you saith, I am of Paul; and I of Apollos; and I of Cephas; and I of Christ." Apollos, the flaming Greek evangelist, had visited Corinth and preached twice there. Some said, "I was saved over in the football stadium when evangelist Apollos was preaching. I'm an Apollos man." Some said, "I'm of Cephas." (That's Simon Peter.) "I'm a Simon Peter man!" And then some pious brother would say, "I've got you all beat—I am of Christ." Can't you just hear it?

"Is Christ divided?" Paul asked. "Was Paul crucified for you? Were you baptized in the name of Paul? Thank God I didn't baptize any of you except Crispus and Gaius."

So the first ill effect of their independence from God was that they had taken their eyes off Jesus. Too much attention was placed on man, and a divisive party spirit resulted.

The second symptom was that they had taken their eyes off the spiritual and put them on carnal, fleshly things. One person was living in incest with his stepmother and was boasting about it! Food and drink were so important, they were stuffing themselves at the Lord's Supper table and even getting drunk there.

As another symptom of their sickness, they had taken their eyes off evangelism. The "sign" gifts, intended to be a sign to unbelievers of the validity of Christ's message, were abused and used on themselves. There's no question they were using the gift of languages in First Corinthians. The question is, were they using it right? Were they *using* it, or *abusing* it? The priority in the church was, unfortunately, to edify itself, to play with the gift of languages among each other instead of out on the mission field, where it was intended. So they had taken their eyes off Christ and put them on man; off the spiritual and on the carnal; off world evangelism and on self-edification.

Fourth, they had taken their eyes off the power of God and put them on human reason. The church was divided, split over the doctrinal issue of the validity of the resurrection. Paul spends a whole chapter dealing with the question that some of them don't even believe in the resurrection of the dead (1 Corinthians 15). Paul says, "If Christ be not risen, then several things follow." One, you're still in your sin; two, the dead are still lost; three, there's no salvation; four, there's no tomorrow; five, Christ is a liar; and six, our hope is in vain. Everything, he says, depends on the resurrection.

Why did the Corinthians disbelieve that? Because they could not logically explain it. They thought themselves supreme. What they could not explain, they would not believe. So Paul prays before their surgery for them to have an understanding of their union in Jesus Christ, saying, "You'll never start to get well from all these abuses of gifts, doctrines, dissension, and apostolic authority until you get back to the central truth of the grace of God— who and what Jesus Christ did for you, and who and what you are in union with Him."

2. "*I thank my God . . . that in everything ye are enriched by him, in all utterance, and in all knowledge*" (v. 5). The city of Corinth was well-known for its educated people. Therefore, when it came to religion, they knew the things of God mentally. They were gifted in "utterance," that is, they could speak the things of God

eloquently with their lips. But they were not experiencing the reality of God's power in their hearts. Paul says to the church at Corinth, you need to understand that because of the sufficiency of Christ, even the least educated among you, who isn't literate and can't even talk plainly, is greater than the most brilliant person who is not in union with Christ.

Note 1 Corinthians 1:26–27: "Ye see your calling, brethren, how that not many wise men after the flesh, not many mighty, not many noble, are called. But God hath chosen the foolish things of the world to confound the wise." Paul says that the sufficiency of Jesus Christ makes even the feeblest of human efforts more profound than the most brilliant thing that someone would say apart from Christ.

3. *"I thank God for the validation of your experience."* Verse 6: "Even as the testimony of Christ was confirmed in you." The Greek text reads, "Our testimony *about* Christ which was confirmed to you."

Paul says, "I want to remind you that our testimony about Christ was validated in you. You yourselves are living, breathing proof that what we told you *would* happen, *did* happen since you had union with Christ." Their lives were a validation of the Word of God, which promised that union with Christ makes the difference.

To what kind of people was Paul saying these things? "Know ye not that the unrighteous shall not inherit the kingdom of God? Be not deceived: neither fornicators, nor idolaters, nor adulterers, nor effeminate, nor abusers of themselves with mankind, nor thieves, nor covetous, nor drunkards, nor revilers, nor extortioners, shall inherit the kingdom of God" (1 Corinthians 6:9–10). Can people like this go to heaven? No! Not in their natural state. The next verse states, "And such *were* some of you." To be in Christ means this is what you *used* to be, *but now* you're washed; *but now* you are sanctified; *but now* you are justified in the name of the Lord Jesus, and by the Spirit of our God."

Yes you, "even you," ought to understand what it means to be a new creation, because of your union with Jesus Christ.

4. *"I thank God for the provision of your gifts."* Verse 7: "So that ye come behind in no gift." I used to think this statement meant that the Corinthians were not current in their tithes and offerings. I even had a good sermon written on it, but I never preached it; I found out that isn't exactly what it means. "So that ye come behind in no gift, waiting for the coming of our Lord Jesus Christ" must be understood by turning these two clauses around so that it reads like this: "So that, waiting for the coming of our Lord Jesus Christ, you realize you come behind in no gift."

Paul writes that the Corinthians were not lacking any of the equipping virtues of the Spirit to serve faithfully while they waited for Jesus' return. This is a rich, profound, important prayer. Paul is praying, "You don't need to be seeking more gifts or arguing about the priority of the gifts; you need to use properly the gifts you already have." He says, "God has equipped you through the Holy Spirit with everything you need to live for Christ in the cesspool of this world till Jesus comes." We should learn to pray with Paul that those we love will appreciate the adequacy of the gifts they are given.

5. *"I thank God that He will confirm you blameless in the day of our Lord Jesus Christ."* Paul says, "You're not only going to endure, but. . . . The basis of the holiness of your life is none other than the returning Christ Himself."

The Greek word "confirm" means to keep strong. "Even you in Corinth don't have to just barely make it by the skin of your teeth, because Christ is the basis of your victory, your sanctification, your holiness." We are *more* than conquerors through Him that loved us and gave Himself for us (Romans 8:37).

The spiritually sick need to understand their victory is not by faith *in* Jesus Christ, but by the faith *of* Jesus. The emphasis is not on faith, but on Christ. I do not simply live out this new life by faith in the Son of God, but by *the* faith of the Son of God. It is Christ who lives in me and lives out His life. I'm not hanging on for dear life; I'm not slipping and sliding, barely holding on to Him. Since He loves me, *He holds* me. That makes all the difference in this world and the world to come.

Paul did not say, "Christ, the hope of glory." He said, "Christ *in you*, the hope of glory." We are not to look philosophically at what Jesus can potentially do, but at what experientially "Christ living in us" is doing right now. The hope for the spiritually sick is "Christ living in them." We need to pray that they will let go of self and let God live in them and through them.

Paul says that we must understand God's sufficiency, which established us at the beginning, His provision of gifts that sustain us while we wait, and the adequacy of His person to confirm us to the very end.

6. *"I thank God for the guarantee of your success."* "God is faithful, by whom ye were called unto the fellowship of his Son Jesus Christ our Lord" (1 Corinthians 1:9). Paul has spoken to them of their standing in grace, their sufficiency in Christ, the validation of their experience, the provision of their gifts, and the basis of their holiness, and concludes with reminding them that he thanks God in prayer for the guarantee of their success.

The first three words of the verse give the entire basis for the good health of the spiritually sick. "God is faithful." Philippians 1:6 expounds this further. "Being confident of this very thing, that He which hath begun a good work in you will perform it [will establish it, will continue to live it out, will finish it, will complete it] until the day of Jesus Christ" (*Amplified*).

The Bible presents salvation as a panorama. Before

131

the worlds were formed, we were foreknown, predestined to be saved; then we were called, we responded and we were justified. We were set apart and made holy and sanctified and kept from a polluted world and finally, in His presence, we will be glorified. This is the *whole* condition of salvation. If we drop out somewhere along the way, it's not salvation. What kind of a guarantee of a trip to Hong Kong is it that promises to get you at least eighty to ninty percent of the way?

The guarantee of the spiritually sick's cure lies in the faithfulness of God. God does the saving, and God does the keeping. What more does a shaky believer need to know than the stability of His adequacy? He who created us, called us, and saved us also keeps us and finishes us in Jesus Christ.

Paul could have begun his letter by rebuking the Corinthians. Sometimes the sheep need to be skinned; but most of the time they need to be loved and fed. Paul thus laid the groundwork for surgery on his spiritually sick children in Christ. His preparation was a prayer of thanksgiving and a prayer of understanding for them. Then they were ready for spiritual surgery, knowing it was to be performed in love.

CHAPTER 16

How to Pray for the Spiritually Whole

(Paul's Prayer for the Thessalonians)

> We give thanks to God always for you all, making
> mention of you in our prayers; Remembering without
> ceasing your work of faith, and labour of love, and
> patience of hope in our Lord Jesus Christ, in the sight
> of God and our Father. (1 Thessalonians 1:2–3)

Unlike the Corinthian congregation, the Thessalonian
church is in relatively good shape. The two letters to the
Thessalonians are encouraging and supportive, while
generally lacking the rebuke to which we have become
accustomed in many of Paul's other writings.

The general theme of Paul's prayers for this church is
to compliment them for the spiritual maturity they have
achieved and encourage them in the great distance they
have yet to go. We will attempt to consolidate and
harmonize into three simple thoughts the fourteen prayers
found in the two letters.

There are three things for which Paul is grateful in the
Thessalonians' lives. They are their work of faith; their
labor of love; and their patience of hope. All the material
to be found in the prayers of 1 and 2 Thessalonians may be
broadly fitted into the framework of these three thoughts.

1. *Their Work of Faith.* The epistle opens in its second and third verses with the sweet reminder that the beloved apostle regularly gives thanks to God for their work of faith. The work of faith may be understood in the New Testament in two senses. There is, first of all, the work of "The Faith." In 1 Timothy 3:9, Paul lists the requirements of a deacon and indicates that a candidate for that high office must hold "the mystery of *the faith* in a pure conscience." In this setting, the expression "the faith" refers to the sum total of all that is contained in the kingdom of Christ. An understanding of its concepts, principles, philosophies, theologies, relationships, priorities, attitudes, and purposes must well be within the grasp of men qualified for spiritual leadership.

In this sense the Thessalonian church was diligent in working *for and in* the faith. He who so serves has a good view of eternal values. The priorities of Christ and His church are his chief concern. The advancement of our Lord's kingdom on earth is the most important factor in his life.

Time would forbid to enumerate the countless laymen whose lives have crossed my path whose priority to our Lord and to His work have been both an inspiration and an unmeasured blessing. The stars of heaven will twinkle brightly with the jewels of crowns won by those who have long and well prioritized the work of "the faith."

Second, the all-embracing concept of "the work of faith" must be understood. The concept means serving God in obedience to His Word with unwavering *trust in His promises.* Everything about the work of the ministry is a work of faith. We plant that others might reap. We sow the seed that God might bring forth the flower in due season. Whatever our hearts lead us to do in His service must be done in faith, believing that God will prosper our efforts in accordance with the promise of His Word. Some men work for fear of retribution that will come if they work not. Others labor merely from a sense of drudgery and duty. Still others, only for the hope of financial gain. But we sow the seed in faith and perform our services all in faith, believing God to honor His Word and bless our efforts out of hearts of boundless love. We must never slacken our efforts as we sow the seed in faith, for we are weaving a garment of praise and honor to our Lord.

Dr. William Barclay tells the story of a minister who repeatedly visited in a home where the young daughter was forever sewing sequins on a gown. "Don't you ever get tired of your work?" the minister asked.

"No, sir," she replied. "I am sewing my wedding dress."

We too, in our work of faith, are weaving a wedding garment in anticipation of the wedding feast with our long-awaited groom.

In 1 Thessalonians 3:9–10, Paul again reminds the Thessalonians that he thanks God regularly in his prayers for the prospect of seeing them soon that he might "perfect that which is lacking in their faith." The word in the Old English expressing "to perfect" means simply "to complete" or "to bring to maturity." The Thessalonians have done well, but are cautioned that excellence in the work of faith does not merit a vacation. The goal for which they strive is far, far away and much work has yet to be done. When we have reached one lost soul, we must reach another. When we have increased our Sunday school class, we must expand it again. Always there is tomorrow. The next hill must ever be climbed . . . the next day's deed accomplished.

The great genius of the Christian life is that our Lord has placed some marvelous possibilities therein. There are mysteries that cannot be understood. There are blessings to be received from a God who cannot be outgiven. There is an ever-anticipated Second Coming we cannot predict, and there are goals we cannot achieve. But we are always to keep striving in spite of the mysteries, and always to keep giving in spite of being outgiven. Just so, we must be ever watching in spite of His delay and ever pressing on in spite of the elusive goal of perfection.

Further, Paul says that our work of faith must be experienced in power. In 2 Thessalonians 1:11 he reminds them again that he prays that God would fulfill all the good pleasure of "the work of faith with power." Paul is reminding the Thessalonians of something we must ever be mindful of. Although we face an impossible task, we must not serve with a sense of drudgery or frustration. The answer? We must labor in the power of the Spirit. The labor of the flesh and the effect of mere human reason will, indeed, quickly lead us to a dead-end street in our quest for the illusive dream. But when such an effort is undertaken in the power of the Holy Spirit, everything is changed.

2. Their "Labor of Love."

Remembering without ceasing your work of faith, and labour of love, and patience of hope in our Lord Jesus Christ, in the sight of God and our Father. (1 Thessalonians 1:3)

No more beautiful expression may describe the service of our Lord than that His children perform a "labor of love." One cannot help but think of myriad ministries performed by the nameless millions in this world whose pictures shall never fill the papers, whose names never make the headlines, but who are the "apples of their Lord's eye." Never quit serving. Keep pressing on to higher ground. The Heavenly Bugler never sounds a retreat. The battle cry is ever and always, "Onward, Christian soldiers." And when we grow dreary, let our mind's eye rush again to Calvary, for there on an old rugged cross hangs the love of God for us. Perfect love requires perfect love in return. Ours is a work of love.

In 1 Thessalonians 3:12, Paul admonishes that their labor of love be greater still. "And the Lord make you to increase and abound in love one toward another and

136

toward all men." Statistics have shown that nine out of ten who enter full-time Christian service at age twenty-one will have dropped out by age sixty-five. The love that motivates us must continue to sustain us. Our love for the Lord must be an abounding one, reaching to others with whom we serve, and to all men whom we would reach. One thing is sure, if we don't really love the Lord, we won't be able to love His children; and if we don't love people, then our displeasure with them will likely become so all-consuming as to cause us to abandon His service. We had better learn to keep Jesus "sweet on our souls" if we intend to continue in service for Him and for those for whom He died.

3. *Their Patience of Hope.* It is this prayer that Paul supports the most with his other prayers. The rest of the fourteen prayers in the two epistles make it obvious that Paul has in mind the eternal plan of God from their election to their ultimate glorification as the Thessalonians are encouraged to wait patiently. Two aspects in the panoramic plan from election to glorification are in view. They are (1) its doctrinal basis; and (2) its personal expression.

In regard to the doctrinal basis of the plan of God, there is election first of all.

> So that we ourselves glory in you in the churches of God for your patience and faith in all your persecutions and tribulations that ye endure. (*2 Thessalonians 1:4*)

The election of God has to do with our beginning. We are elected by God to start. But starting is not all. Finishing is everything, and we are therefore chosen unto salvation.

> But we are bound to give thanks alway to God for you, brethren beloved of the Lord, because God hath from the beginning chosen you to salvation through sanc-

tification of the Spirit and belief of the truth. (2 Thessalonians 2:13)

Many evangelicals err in their understanding of "salvation" as simply being "saved." Salvation means "I have been saved from the penalty of sin, I am being saved from the power of sin, and I will yet be saved from the presence of sin." In election we began the course in salvation, in glorification it is finished. But keep in focus that the entire process is based on our reception of the Word (1 Thessalonians 2:13).

Our response to God's election must be a response of faith. And how is faith produced? "Faith cometh by hearing, and hearing by the word of God" (Romans 10:17). Our Lord clearly taught that Satan is eager to snatch away the Word. Paul is grateful that the Word has been gladly received by the Thessalonians, for their response of faith was necessary to make their calling and election sure. We must earnestly pray that the Word that goes from our lips shall be received and mixed with faith as it is heard by those with whom we share.

There is the guarantee of the ultimate blamelessness of the whole being (1 Thessalonians 5:23). At the very end, the spirit, soul, and body will have been preserved by the Lord Jesus Christ, either by our translation at His appearance or by our glorification at the resurrection at His coming. We shall ultimately be "like Him," for we shall see Him as He is. This is the guarantee of the Spirit to us and part of that for which Paul thanks God.

Then there is the practical side of Paul's prayer for the Thessalonians in regard to their continued patience and hope. From conversion to heaven, the believer waits patiently in hope of the final transformation of the entire being into the image of God's Son. The doctrinal basis of this hope has been seen in God's election and choice and through man's reception of the Word with the consummate guarantee of ultimate blamelessness. Paralleling the

138

doctrine basis of our hope is man's responsibility. The doctrinal basis of our hope is God's part. The practical expression is man's part.

Paul prays that the Thessalonians might be faithful in their personal expression of this hope in their personal lives. Four things are the subsequent object of his prayer in their behalf. There is, first, the sanctification of the heart (1 Thessalonians 3:10–13).

The prayer of Paul in this passage is the establishment of the heart unto holiness before the Lord. Interestingly, the Hebrews had no word for the expression "sanctify." The concept, therefore, was stated as "holifying" the Lord in the heart, to set aside the heart, to holify it, to sanctify it completely to the Lord.

The heart is the seat of emotion and desire. Our Lord taught, "set your affection on things above, not on things on the earth" (Colossians 3:2). The decision to set God apart and His will as the priority of our desires is a willful decision of the heart of man. God cannot do it for us. To will our own sanctification is a decision of the heart and can only be done by the expression of our own volition.

The ultimate result of such a prior commitment, then, becomes quite naturally a life worthy of His calling (2 Thessalonians 1:11). This expression means that the believer is to so live that Christ may be seen in his life. That the personality of the Lord Jesus might be seen in his life must ever be the goal of the one who has sanctified God in his heart. Our lives must be worthy of the name they bear. The world should never be surprised to observe our lives and later find we bear the name of Christ.

In such a manner of living, we therefore fulfill His goodness.

> Wherefore also we pray always for you, that our God would count you worthy of this calling, and fulfill all the good pleasure of his goodness, and the work of faith with power. (2 Thessalonians 1:11)

Paul prays for the Thessalonians to so live as to fulfill all the good pleasure of His goodness. If there is one simple expression that may adequately describe the nature of God in comprehensive, human terminology, it is simply that "God is a good God." Perhaps nothing better reflects the personality of the Father through us than that the world would look at us and say, "Now, there is a good man." In so doing, we will fulfill the last practical expression for which Paul prays, that being that the Lord Jesus Christ may be glorified in us.

At the heart of every decision is a simple criteria: Does it glorify God? The Westminster Catechism has adequately defined the purpose of man: "To glorify God and enjoy Him forever."

Doctrinally God has done His part in guaranteeing man's election, salvation, and ultimate blamelessness of the whole being. Practically we are to so live as to sanctify God in the heart, which results in living a worthy life, fulfilling His goodness, and glorifying His name.

Far too few are the churches like the one in Thessalonica, for which one could be eternally grateful for such spiritual characteristics. Where they are found, gratitude is to be given and encouragement made to press on to perfection, that nothing might lack in the spiritual maturity of the whole man in Christ. Where it does not exist, the decision must be made today to begin. God has positionally guaranteed it; we must practically begin to experience it. The first step is to set God apart in our hearts, as Lord of all, holifying—sanctifying—our whole being to Him. This is Paul's prayer for the Thessalonian church, and this should be our prayer for ourselves and our own.

CHAPTER 17

The Master's Prayer Life

The songwriter has expressed the prayer of our hearts in the lovely hymn "More Like the Master." Peter taught that we can and should be like Jesus.

> For even hereunto were ye called: because Christ also suffered for us, leaving us an example, that ye should follow his steps. (1 Peter 2:21)

As in all things, Jesus is our example in prayer. In Luke 22:41 we are told that Jesus knelt down to pray. Never are we more like Him than when we do the same. We are to kneel reverently as did Solomon in the temple. We are to bow before Him, as did Abram at Bethel; and Moses at Sinai; as did Elijah at Carmel; and Jonah at Nineveh.

We must kneel in conversion, as did Paul; in honor, as did the soldiers at the cross; and at death, as did Stephen.

But above all things, we are, like the Master, to pray. The earthly ministry of our Lord was begun in prayer: "Now when all the people were baptized, it came to pass, that Jesus also being baptized, and praying, the heaven was opened" (Luke 3:21). The earthly life of our Lord was consummated in prayer: "Then said Jesus, Father forgive them; for they know not what they do. And they parted his raiment, and cast lots" (Luke 23:34).

When we pray, Satan trembles. When we pray, the Evil One flees and trials pale before us as the grass withers before the scorching sun at noontime. When we pray, the power comes, love fills our heart, and all of life is filled with song.

There is glorious privilege in prayer. The songwriter William W. Walford said it well for us.

> Sweet hour of prayer, sweet hour of prayer
> That calls me from a world of care,
> And bids me at my Father's throne
> Make all my wants and wishes known:
> In seasons of distress and grief
> My soul has often found relief,
> And oft escaped the tempter's snare
> By thy return, sweet hour of prayer.
>
> Sweet hour of prayer, sweet hour of prayer,
> Thy wings shall my petition bear
> To Him whose truth and faithfulness
> Engage the waiting soul to bless:
> And since He bids me seek His face,
> Believe His Word, and trust His grace,
> I'll cast on Him my every care,
> And wait for thee, sweet hour of prayer.

A brief survey of the Master's prayer life will reveal the following:

1. He Prayed in Secret.

And when he had sent the multitudes away, he went up into a mountain apart to pray: and when the evening was come, he was there alone. (Matthew 14:23)

The physical closet of prayer, as well as that of the heart, is imperative to a healthy prayer life. Prayer must become habitual. "To pray without ceasing" means to be in a constant attitude of the divine presence. But nothing will substitute for the habitual practice of prayer in a secret place. Here our Lord's example must be meticulously followed.

2. He Never Allowed a Busy Schedule to Keep Him From Prayer.

> And it came to pass, when he was in a certain city, behold a man full of leprosy: who seeing Jesus fell on his face, and besought him, saying, Lord, if thou wilt, thou canst make me clean. And he put forth his hand, and touched him, saying, I will: be thou clean. And immediately the leprosy departed from him. And he charged him to tell no man: but go, and shew thyself to the priest, and offer for they cleansing, according as Moses commanded, for a testimony unto them. But so much the more went there a fame abroad of him: and great multitudes came together to hear, and to be healed by him of their infirmities. And he withdrew himself into the wilderness, and prayed. *(Luke 5:12–16)*

If we will, we may take time to pray. The problem is not that we have no time to pray, but that we have no desire.

3. He Prayed Early in the Morning.

> And in the morning, rising up a great while before day, he went out, and departed into a solitary place, and there prayed. *(Mark 1:35)*

The Lord has promised, "They that seek me early shall find me." Following His example, we will find that the sweetness of the early hours are the best.

4. He Prayed Before He Ate.

And Jesus took the loaves; and when he had given thanks, he distributed to the disciples, and the disciples to them that were set down; and likewise of the fishes as much as they would. (John 6:11)

5. He Prayed Before the Important Events of His Life.

These words spake Jesus, and lifted up his eyes to heaven, and said, Father, the hour is come; glorify thy Son, that thy Son also may glorify thee: As thou hast given him power over all flesh, that he should give eternal life to as many as thou hast given him. And this is life eternal, that they might know thee the only true God, and Jesus Christ, whom thou hast sent. I have glorified thee on the earth: I have finished the work which thou gavest me to do. (John 17:1–4)

6. He Prayed in Times of Great Popularity.

Then those men, when they had seen the miracle that Jesus did, said, This is of a truth that prophet that should come into the world. When Jesus therefore perceived that they would come and take him by force, to make him a king, he departed again into a mountain himself alone. (John 6:14–15)

7. He Prayed in Times of Complete Rejection.

Then cometh Jesus with them unto a place called Gethsemane, and saith unto the disciples, Sit ye here, while I go and pray yonder. And he took with him Peter and the two sons of Zebedee, and began to be sorrowful and very heavy. Then saith he unto them, My soul is exceeding sorrowful, even unto death: tarry ye here, and watch with me. (Matthew 26:36–38)

8. He Prayed Submissively.

And he went a little farther, and fell on his face, and prayed, saying, O my Father, if it be possible, let this cup pass from me: nevertheless not as I will, but as thou wilt. (Matthew 26:39)

9. He Prayed for His Enemies.

Then said Jesus, Father, forgive them; for they know not what they do. And they parted his raiment, and cast lots. *(Luke 23:34)*

10. He Prayed Earnestly.

And being in an agony he prayed more earnestly: and his sweat was as it were great drops of blood falling down to the ground. *(Luke 22:44)*

Jesus was our model and teacher in prayer. By His life and His lips the Lord's constant fellowship with His Father pointed to the necessity of ours. If *He* must pray, how much more ought we to pray, and that with all our hearts.

CHAPTER 18

Jesus' High Priestly Prayer

Jesus' prayer in John 17 is truly "the Lord's Prayer." The Model Prayer commonly called the Lord's Prayer was a prayer that Jesus taught as an example when His disciples asked, "Lord, teach us how to pray." But John 17 records Jesus' own prayer. It should probably be called "Jesus' High Priestly Prayer."

This is the classic prayer of the Bible. It is Jesus at His most earnest, praying out of His heart. It includes the entire seventeenth chapter of the Gospel of John. Jesus as our Great High Priest is performing the function of a priest. He is interceding for His own. He is praying for others. He is praying for His people. Actually, it may or may not have been prayed in the garden where He prayed, "Thy will be done." It appears chronologically that this prayer was, rather, spoken on the way to the garden.

We can learn much about the heart of God and how He would have us to pray for ourselves, our churches, and our fellow Christians by listening to how Jesus prayed in our behalf. In this prayer there are four things for which He intercedes for His own.

1. He Prays for His Father's Glory. Verse one begins, "These words spake Jesus, and lifted up his eyes to heaven." Possibly the expression, "these words spake Jesus," should be followed by a period and be the close of chapter 16. This marks the end of the *teachings* of Jesus. From here on we have an account of what *happened* to Jesus.

Now chapter 17 changes the subject and might begin, "And Jesus lifted up his eyes to heaven." He is not just speaking words. He is praying to His Father, and there is a vast difference in the chronology as well as the import of these events.

Jesus prays, "Father, the hour is come. This is what we planned for and waited for." Some liberal theologians have suggested that the Cross was an accident where everything got out of hand. They say God never intended for His Son to die. But that is not true.

Jesus Christ was the Lamb slain from the foundation of the world (Revelation 13:8). Before Jesus was born, before there was a sinful race to redeem, before there was a devil to tempt man, before there was anything, God planned His creation. He knew it would fall, and He planned its redemption in the heart of the Father, Son, and Holy Spirit. In the mind of the Father, it was as good as done. Jesus Christ was as good as dead. Slain from the foundation of the world, He prayed, "The hour is come. The time is at hand. That which we have planned, and which I have been willing to suffer from the foundation of the world, is now upon us." What is the essence of the whole thing? It is, "Glorify thy Son, that thy Son also may glorify thee" (v. 1).

Had Jesus Christ not gone to the cross, the greatest thing the world has ever known—the amazing grace of the gospel, the wonder of the scheme of redemption where God's Lamb was slain on Golgotha's bloody brow—would never have happened. Nothing in all the world ever brought glory to the Father like the expression of His love in His Son on the cross. Jesus said, "Father, if I don't do it and we don't go through with what we have planned, lost man cannot be redeemed. Not one sinner will ever glorify you."

That is why we sing, "In the cross of Christ I glory." That is why we proclaim, "That which to the Gentiles is foolishness, and that which to the Jews is a stumbling block, ridiculous to the pagan, unbelieving, pseudointellectual, humanistic society, the *cross* is to us the glory of God. The most wonderful, glorious thing God has ever done is to plan the scheme of redemption by which He would reconcile men to Himself through forgiveness provided in the death of His Son on the old rugged cross.

"Father, if I don't do this, not one soul will ever glorify you." Lost sinners don't glorify God. It is because of redemption that we can stand and sing "Amazing Grace," "All Hail the Power," "The King Is Coming," "To God Be the Glory," "In the Cross of Christ I Glory." The glory of God is and was and shall ever be central in the mind of the Lord Jesus Christ.

The perfect life Jesus had lived gave efficacy to His death. The expression "We are saved by His life" means that if He had not lived a perfect life, there would be no vicarious nature to His death for a sinful substitute, and an imperfect Savior could not die on our behalf. The purpose of His perfect life was to give meaning to His death.

"Glorify thou me with thine own self with the glory which I had with thee before the world was" (v. 5). What glory would there be to God if not one sinner was ever converted? "Therefore, if I am to know glory, if men are to give glory, if I am to glorify you, and if you are to be glorified, then that for which all my perfect life prepared me must become an effective reality on the cross."

The first sixty-five books of the Bible present Christ in His humiliation. The last presents Him in His exaltation. Revelation is the answer to this prayer of Jesus to receive back His glory. And *how* He gets it back! But He had to go

148

to the cross to do it. The Lamb slain in Luke is the Lamb exalted in Revelation. The scheme of redemption for which He prayed, and the courage and strength to go through it from the foundation of the world, was and is the ultimate manifestation of the glory of God. Remember this—God's ultimate glory is not in His healing power; not in His prophetic statements; not in His miracles; not in His philosophical utterances; not in His matchless teachings. It is in His death on Calvary to reconcile sinners Himself. God did the one act that most completely glorifies Him in the cross of Christ. So He begins with a prayer for His Father's glory.

2. *He Prays for His Friends.* He is praying for us (vv. 6–19). "I have manifested thy name unto the men which thou gavest me out of the world." Jesus came to manifest, amplify, and augment the name of God to the world. "Thine they were [they were yours, you planned for their redemption], and thou gavest them me; and they have kept thy word" (v. 6). The only way we can be saved is to keep His Word. We hear the Word, we believe the Word, we respond to the Word.

Verse 7: "Now they have known that all things whatsoever thou hast given me are of thee." How do they know? They have believed the Word. How will we ever know that Jesus Christ is the Son of God? By experiencing His Word. He said, "You shall find me when you seek for me with all your heart" and "He that cometh unto me I will in no wise cast out." If we believe His Word and respond to His Word—not an emotional jag, not a philosophical concept, not a church ordinance—but His Word, then we will know that Jesus Christ is God's Son. He blesses His Word, and He blesses our response to His Word. The experience follows the Word. People say that if they had a great experience, they would believe. Jesus says, "If you believe, you will have a great experience" on the basis of His Word.

Verse 8: "For I have given unto them the words which thou gavest me." This is not just something man has made up. This is the Word of the Father. . . . "And they have received them, and have known surely that I came out from thee, and they have believed that thou didst send me." Therefore, "I pray for them." Jesus reminds the Father that in response to His Word, they have believed. Therefore, the Father's responsibility to them is to honor and to keep His Word.

The next six words are very interesting. "I pray not for the world" (v. 9). He's praying for those who have believed God's Word. I do not find anywhere in the Bible that we are told specifically to pray for the lost. Yet the apostle Paul says, "I would that you pray for kings and for all in places of authority" (see 1 Timothy 2:1–2). How can this be reconciled? By understanding that we are to pray for ourselves that God will make us the salt of the earth, that spiritual men will be in high places making spiritual decisions. God promises, "If my people, which are called by my name, will humble themselves and pray, I will hear from heaven, forgive their sins, and heal their land" (see 2 Chronicles 7:14).

We know this to be true. God wants to give revival. But the emphasis is never on the secular system, on society. We know from the Book of Revelation that this world system is under the condemnation of God. It can't be redeemed, and it won't be redeemed. Things won't be turned around. We are to pray for ourselves, and we are witnesses to the world. We are to preach to the world. We are to tell the gospel to the world, but this world system has had its day. Regardless of who gets elected president, nothing is going to change the world system. So let's keep a good balance that enables us to pray for spiritual insight by our leaders.

We are to pray for revival among the believers. Why? That we might witness the gospel because it is the Word of God which opens the hearts of men and causes them to be saved. It is important that Jesus says, "I am not praying for the system of this world. "But," He says, "I do pray for them which thou has given me." "They are My concern." If you and I who are the salt of the earth would just pray for ourselves, be full of the Spirit, and spread the Word, the world would be transformed.

The world is not the problem; we are the problem. We need to be praying for ourselves, our righteousness, our life, and our witness that we may indeed be the salt of the earth.

Verse 10: "All mine are thine, and thine are mine; and I am glorified in them." Verse 11: "And now I am no more in the world." Lord, I'm leaving; I'm coming to thee; I am coming back; but, Lord, they have got to stay down here. "Holy Father, keep through thine own name."

The name of God is the ultimate validation of the authority and Word of God. Jesus says, "I am pleading with you—I invoke you by your own name, by that which is changeless. . . . I am leaving them whom thou hast given me, that they may be one as we are." Even now Jesus is seated at the right hand of the Father. And what is He doing? He ever lives to make intercession for His own. He is still interceding for us.

Verse 12: "While I was with them in the world, I kept them in thy name: Lord, those that thou gavest me I have kept, and none of them is lost, but the son of perdition; that the scripture might be fulfilled." Jesus knew beforehand that, the last time He was to pray with three of them, they would fall asleep. "Oh, they are so weak, Lord, they didn't even live for you very well when I was here in the body, and now I'm leaving. Oh, Father, you've got to help them." What pathos and agony and empathy for us is in the heart of Christ as He pleads with the Father for us!

"For their sake, I sanctify myself, I set myself aside for them, Lord, for the holy purpose of the cross that they also might be sanctified through the truth. I will give myself for them, Father, but then I must leave them. Now through the truth of your Word, keep them." How beautifully our Lord prays for His own! How wonderful to know both day or night He who never slumbers or sleeps is at the right hand of the Father every second of every minute of every hour of every day of every month of every year of every century, praying for us from the cradle to the grave! I am thankful that He prays for His friends, and so ought we to be.

3. *He Prays for the Future.* Verse 20: "Neither pray I for these alone, but for them also which shall believe on me through their word." Keep in mind that Jesus says, "I am not praying for an unbelieving world." Rather, "I am praying for those which are in the world who are yet to be saved." Why? Because Jesus Christ, as God, had an eternal view of things. He was never bound by the limitations and the small perspective of time and space. He was the Lamb slain from the foundation of the world, not yet experientially, but positionally—in the mind of God eternally as good as done. He said, "I sent them into the world." He hadn't given them the Great Commission yet, but in the mind of God it was positionally done, thought yet experientially to be done after Jesus' resurrection.

Now what is Jesus saying? He is saying that salvation is predestined from the foundation of the world. In His mind the elect, though still lost, are as good as saved. They are predestined to be saved. They are in the world, but they are not of the world. They are the redeemed who are yet to be called out of the world. The eternal perspective of Jesus who is "the same yesterday, today, and forever." God incarnate, the great I AM, transcends all time and space. Jesus is praying and thanking God for those who will yet be saved, and who He knows will be saved, and who in His mind, though not experientially yet, are positionally as good as saved.

Verse 24 includes them all. "Father, I will that they also whom thou hast given me, be with me where I am."

Jesus has already prayed for those whom He was given by the Father, the ones who have followed Him already; now He prays for the ones who aren't even born yet, who are yet to be saved because of the witness of His own. They all are included in those He has been given. "Father, I pray that they be with me where I am." Didn't He say, "In my Father's house are many mansions; I go to prepare a place for you. And if I go and prepare a place for you, I will come again, and receive you unto myself; that where I am, there ye may be also" (John 14:2–3)?

In heaven we shall see "the glory that God has given Him." We haven't seen it yet. "You remember how you loved me before the foundation of the world and how the manifestation of your love was to my honor and glory. You loved to glorify the Son as the Son loved to glorify you. Father, it is going to be that way again like it used to be in heaven from the foundation of the world, and I want them to see it, and share it with us."

Verses 25–26: "Righteous Father, the world hath not known me; they did not know who I was, but I've known you, Father, and these have known that thou hath sent me, so they know me and you. And I declared unto them thy name. I revealed your glory and will declare that the love wherewith thou hath loved me may be in them and I in them" (author's paraphrase). So the glory of His Father, revealed through those who through His Son's death will come to know Him, is again the burden of His prayer as He consummates His prayer.

5. *He Prays for Their Fellowship.* "And now I am no more in the world, but these are in the world" (v. 11). They have to stay here, even though I am coming to you. "Holy Father, keep through thine own name those whom thou hast given me, that they *may be one,* as we are." Jesus prays that we might be one, in the same way He is: The Father, the Son, and the Spirit, three persons yet so completely one as to be a mystery. Though you and I as

153

His disciples, as believers, are individual personalities, distinct individuals, yet we are all one as well.

Verse 21 picks up the same theme. "[I pray] that they all may be one; as thou, Father, art in me, and I in thee, that they also may be one in us." Why is Jesus praying that we may be one? *In order that the world may believe that thou hast sent me."* The primary reason for blessings of God on any church is its unity, its oneness in Jesus Christ.

Why is unity important? Jesus Christ gives us two things through His Spirit. First, He gives fruit. The fruit of the Spirit are manifestations of His personality. Second, He gives gifts. The body-edifying type of gifts manifest His ministry. So as we exercise our various gifts in love, in honor preferring one another, do you know what happens? *You and I, as His church, become the continual reincarnation of the body of Jesus Christ.* Every time His body comes together, the Spirit joins us to the Head in heaven. Therefore, as a harmonious body of Christ on earth, we have been His continuing reincarnation for twenty centuries of what the temporary incarnation was in a different kind of body for thirty-three years. He prayed for the Father's glory, for His friends, for future believers, and for our fellowship. What a perfect example for our prayer life!

CHAPTER 19

How to Pray to the Father

(The Lord's Prayer)

> And it came to pass, that, as he was praying in a
> certain place, when he ceased, one of his disciples said
> unto him, Lord, teach us to pray, as John also taught
> his disciples. (*Luke 11:1*)

It was a common sight in Israel to see a religious teacher
giving out a model prayer. Jesus was a teacher. When
Nicodemus confronted Him, he paid Him the ultimate
compliment that a teacher would to another teacher. The
spiritual leaders of Israel were called rabbis or teachers, and
they were also called masters—teaching masters. So, for
one to be called master or teacher or rabbi was really to say
the same thing.

As a master teacher, Nicodemus recognized something in Jesus, however, that was quite different. He said,
"Master, you are a teacher come from God. You are
especially anointed, sent from God." It was one master
teacher recognizing in another that he had an excellence
that made him a cut above the average.

One of the intriguing things that these teachers did
was to teach their little set of disciples how to pray a
special kind of prayer. It was traditional that each rabbi

would try to tailor a special prayer that embraced everything he felt and knew about God. Then he would sum it up in one or two sentences and teach all his disciples to memorize and pray it. It gave more than spiritual unity. It gave a kind of geographical or sociological identity. The prayer the rabbi taught his people to pray made each fellowship distinct from the others. One could be anywhere in the world and hear someone praying a prayer and recognize exactly where he was from.

In this context, one day Jesus' disciples decided they too needed a prayer. "Master, teach us to pray, as John also taught his disciples." They always wanted to be like the others. "We want a king; the world has a king." "We want a deliverer like the Roman Empire's deliverers." They modeled themselves after not only the secular world, but also the religious world. So Jesus taught them to pray the Model Prayer, or the Lord's Prayer. The Gospels record more than one version, but they are essentially the same.

The one that we memorize and find the most familiar is the version recorded in Matthew 6:9–13. "After this manner therefore pray ye: Our Father which art in heaven, Hallowed be thy name. Thy kingdom come. Thy will be done in earth, as it is in heaven. Give us this day our daily bread. And forgive us our debts, as we forgive our debtors. And lead us not into temptation, but deliver us from evil: For thine is the kingdom, and the power, and the glory, for ever. Amen."

This beautiful, significant Lord's Prayer should be understood primarily in terms of two parts, each having three basic ingredients.

The first half of the prayer is "Our Father which art in heaven, Hallowed be thy name. Thy kingdom come. Thy will be done in earth, as it is in heaven." Notice that everything in this part of the prayer focuses on God. Nothing is said about man. Nothing is said about the family of the human race. Nothing is said about the disciples—only about the Father.

156

This first part gives special focus and attention to the Lord's name, His kingdom, and His will. One must begin with an attitude of prayer that has the right concept of God, His kingdom, and His will. For we are not ready to position ourselves rightly to God, to others, or to ourselves until first we have rightly positioned God in our minds.

Most of us come to God with our interests and our needs first. "Lord, give us this day our daily bread. Forgive us our sins. Meet our needs. Bless us. Help Uncle Charlie who's sick, and bless me as well." That's where we start, and that's usually where we end.

But we are not ready to consider our own needs until first they are presented in the proper perspective of God. We must be first concerned about the holiness of the name of God and the kingdom of God, the cause for which God is concerned and the will of God on earth. Then and then alone are we ready to turn to our needs, our causes, our interests, and our will. Doing so will enable His will to become ours.

Once we have established that, we can look at the second half of the prayer. "Give us this day or daily bread, and forgive us our debts, as we forgive our debtors. And lead us not into temptation, but deliver us from evil." As there are three things in the first half that relate to God— His name, His kingdom, and His will—so are there three things in the second part of the prayer that relate to us. There is, first, the problem of the past—"Forgive us the sins of the past." Then, since we live in today, we pray for "daily bread," today's needs. Finally there is tomorrow, the future, so we pray that He will lead us aright, "not into temptation, but deliver us from evil." So in the last half of the prayer, all of man's need are presented in a prospective panorama of life—yesterday, today, and tomorrow.

The First Half. Jesus first speaks of "our Father who is in heaven." The pronoun "our" is used throughout the prayer. As His children we have a distinctive relationship with God "our" Father, and a distinctive responsibility to "our" fellowmen. There is not one mention of the word "I" or "me" or "mine," every emphasis is on "ours." We are praying for ourselves, but also for the family of God. As children of God we are part of a family. We are to pray for the corporate needs of our fellowmen. Every time we pray or sing or read this prayer, *think* about this prayer. Remember the corporate emphasis here on the whole family of God.

Our Father which art in heaven. Give us this day *our* daily bread. Forgive us *our* debts as we forgive *our* debtors. Lead *us* not into temptation. Deliver *us* from evil. Always there is the corporate attention that is focused with the opening word "our."

There is never a Sunday morning when my staff and I assemble for a staff meeting and prayer time that we do not include in our prayers, "O God, bless your church everywhere." Bless the Park Place Church; bless Tallowood; bless Second Church; bless First Methodist Church; bless the missionaries. Do you realize how large the family of God is? I have spent some wonderful Sunday mornings in thatch huts and under stilt houses in Africa. Sometimes I have stood in mud halfway up to my knees with the people of God, half-clothed, ragged, poor, and waiting for the poverty truck to distribute free milk after the service so that the people can live another day. I think about them and other people in all denominations and all churches and all conditions around the world. There is a strong "our" emphasis in the Lord's Prayer; there is nothing said about "me" or "I" or "myself." The perfect prayer, the Model Prayer, first of all gives right attention to God and then right attention to the family of God. In positioning these two things, our personal needs fall into place.

The second part of the first half of this prayer is the word "Father." The word that is used here is *Abba*. It is used by the tiniest little child in Israel who sits on his daddy's knee and puts out his chubby little hands and reaches up and hugs him, kisses him, and calls him the most endearing, intimate word, *Abba*. The nearest translation we have in English is "Daddy." That's almost sacrilegious, isn't it? But that is the only word in the English language that comes close to what *Abba* means. Jesus is teaching us to think of God as the most intimate, understanding, loving heavenly Father.

A Roman emperor was returning from war. As was the custom, he rode in the lead chariot in parade. Suddenly his little five-year-old boy jumped down from the reviewing stand, ran between the legs of the guard, and jumped up on the side of the chariot. One of the big guards picked him up and said, "Son, you can't come up here. He's the Emperor." The little boy said, "Well, he may be *your* emperor, but he's *my* daddy." The father pushed the guard gently aside, and picked the boy up and hugged him. God wants us to think of Him like that.

God wants us to understand Him as an intimate, loving heavenly Father. But intimacy must not breed familiarity and, ultimately, contempt. So immediately Jesus adds, "Hallowed be thy name." This means "made holy" which in turn means that something is unique. It is unlike anything else. It is set aside. It is sacred. It is holy for a special purpose. God is not like anyone else or anything else. Therefore, His name is not like anything else, for it describes the totality of His being.

The Lord's Day is not like any other day and so it is a holy day. The Bible is not like any other book, so it is a holy book. So sanctified, special, unique, one of a kind, set aside, different is the name of God that we pray, "Hallowed be thy name." Immediately following the familiarity and the intimacy of a loving Abba, heavenly Father, Jesus teaches us to pray, "Hallowed be thy name."

Jesus goes on to say, "Thy kingdom come"—period. "Thy will be done in earth as it is in heaven"—period. These are separate sentences, using a common device of the Greek for emphasis by saying essentially the same thing twice.

What is the kingdom of God? A kingdom is a place where the laws, rules, and desires of the king are lived by, honored, and obeyed. The place where the kingdom comes is therefore the place where His will is done.

There are three senses of the kingdom of heaven. It was, it is, and it will yet be. God was in heaven. Apparently Lucifer rebelled against the King and was banished to the earth. So the integrity of heaven is preserved as a place where the King is honored, His laws obeyed, and His will performed. When Jesus walked on the earth, He said the kingdom of God is "within you." When we open our hearts to the King, we become subjects of the King and God recreates the kingdom inside our souls. In this sense the kingdom of God is in the hearts of believers because the King is there.

Then there is the sense in which the kingdom of God is yet to be. That's during the Millennium. For a thousand wonderful years of peace the world will see what the kingdom of God is all about. It will be a kingdom of forced rule. There will be no option to keeping the laws of the King. For a thousand years the kingdom will come on earth in fulfillment of this prayer.

Every time we pray the Lord's Prayer and mean it, we are praying for two things. We pray for world evangelism, for missions, for men to be saved that the King might come and live in their hearts; and we also pray for the return of Jesus and the millennial reign of Christ on earth.

But there's a fourth sense in which the kingdom of God is yet even beyond that. After the millennial reign, the earth and the elements will be dissolved with a fervent heat. Then eternity begins forever, and the kingdom of heaven will last forever.

The preamble of the Constitution to the Kingdom was laid down in the Sermon on the Mount (Matthew 5–7), of which the Lord's Prayer is a a part. The preamble is found in the Beatitudes. Nine times the preamble says "blessed." Blessed means happy. The purpose of the kingdom is to help people to be happy by loving and doing the will of the King. The will of the King is happiness for those in His kingdom.

The Second Half. The second part of the Lord's Prayer is for our personal needs. "Give us this day our daily bread." What does Jesus mean by "our daily bread"? Some suggest it means taking the Eucharist, the Lord's Supper, every single day. That is not likely. Others suggest Jesus is talking primarily about Himself, and that is a beautiful interpretation, for He is indeed our Daily Bread. We must, like the Israelites, faithfully gather the manna.

But very likely Jesus refers to our daily physical food. Surely He wants us to be constantly aware that both spiritual and physical daily bread come from Him. Back of the loaf is the snowy flour; back of the flour, the mill; and back of the mill are the wheat and the rain and the sun and the Father's will. Behind even our daily bread there is provision by the Father.

It is possible to live a whole life and never pray this prayer and still have plenty of food to eat. But it is not likely that we will become the people we are capable of becoming until we first get a grasp of God who is supplying our daily provision of food.

"Forgive us our trespasses." From the Greek, this has been interchangeably interpreted "trespasses," "sins," and "debts." All these words are good translations. There are four Greek words translated "sin" in the New Testament. *Parabasis* means to step across the line. *Paratoma* means that one just slips accidentally across the line. *Anomia* means deliberate rebellion. *Ophelama* means to repay a debt. The word Jesus chooses here teaches us that we have to pay back our debts so that the debt against God might be forgiven. It is imperative that we not judge another person so harshly as to think them unforgivable, regardless of what they have done against us. If we fail to forgive, God will not forgive us.

161

Charles Allen tells in his book *God's Psychiatry* of an episode of "Amos and Andy," the old radio serial, in which Amos says, "Kingfish is always slapping me on the back, and I'm getting tired of it. But I'm going to get even with him. I'm strapping a piece of dynamite to my back, and the next time he whaps me, I'm going to blow his hand off."

If we hold grudges, we only hurt ourselves more than we hurt others. It we won't forgive somebody else, we can't be forgiven. In holding the grudge of unforgiveness against somebody else, we don't do anything but blow ourselves up with our own inability to *receive* forgiveness: That dynamite blows both ways, and that unforgiveness *flows* both ways as well. So when we judge others, we must remember that we're not God. Let God judge. Forgive, and we will be forgiven.

Then Jesus says, "Lead us not into temptation, but deliver us from evil." Are we to understand that we have to ask God, who cannot be tempted of evil, not to lead us into temptation? No. The Greek word translated "temptation" here is the word *paradzi*, which means trial. We are to pray, "Lord, don't be too hard on me. Remember I'm human. Don't put more trial on me than I can bear, and keep me from evil."

The word "evil" means here "the Evil One." There are three Greek words that may be translated "evil one," and this means the one who accuses me. Every time I get into a mess, every time something goes wrong, the Devil says, "Look what happened to him. He's in trouble because of some bad thing that he did." So Jesus teaches us to pray that the Evil One will be silenced and that God may be trusted that He alone leads us into situations that test us and try us.

In such cases the trial will never be more than we can bear. His grace will be sufficient. So we pray, "Lead us not into deep trial." "Don't be too hard on us, Lord. Don't get me into such a mess that the Evil One could accuse me and say I'm in trouble because of my evil. Please test me and try me as a father corrects his child. You please set the perimeters so the accusations of the Evil One will mean nothing. That way you'll know and I'll know that it's a test to make me strong and I can endure it."

Finally Jesus says, "For thine is the kingdom, and the power, and the glory, for ever." This expression is like our saying, "In Jesus' name, Amen." It was put on the end of every Hebrew prayer. It is a kind of benediction or closing. And it is very important. We began with a focus on the kingdom of God and the King of the kingdom. We reviewed the panorama of our human need. Then we closed by bringing into focus again that it is all for the sake and honor of the King and His kingdom. "For it's your kingdom, Lord, and it's up to you to sustain me as a citizen of that kingdom. By the way, Lord, it's your power that helps me stand in the kingdom, in the trial of this world, and Lord, it's for your glory, so please help me."

It is a prayer of beautiful dependence on the Father that first positions the Lord and then ourselves as citizens of His kingdom.

CHAPTER 20

The Name of Jesus

(The One to Whom We Pray)

We cannot overstate our appreciation for the sincerity of Charismatics. It is my conviction that sincere Charismatic people have fallen short in sound biblical exegesis. Healing, tongues, and the baptism in the Holy Spirit are at the heart of their movement.

One could wish to hear more of the Lord Jesus and less of those things. From beginning to end, He is the Word made flesh, incarnate God, and our coming Savior. It is our prayer that all that He is, has been, and forever shall be may abide at the focal point of every doctrine, every theological persuasion, every movement, every church, and every denomination until He returns in glory.

"IN THE BEGINNING WAS THE WORD"

He was
sent from God the Father to the bosom of Mary
the seed of woman
the perfect sacrifice
for sinful man.

He assumed our humanity
to give us His divinity.

He who knew no sin
was made sin
was made a curse
for our sin.

He was rich
but became poor
that through His poverty
we might be rich.

He gave up heaven
His Father's house
with many mansions
Where . . .
the wind never blows
the rain never falls
the flowers never fade
no one is ever sick
or dies,

To come to earth
where He lived in poverty
and was
reared in obscurity
rejected by His own family
doubted by John the Baptist
misunderstood by His disciples
envied by the scribes
despised by the hypocrites
admired by the women
feared by Jewish leaders
betrayed by Judas—and
denied by Peter.

As the baby Jesus
He
was loved by Mary and Joseph
was visited by shepherds
shook up a king
was ignored by the chief priests
was worshiped by the wise men
was dedicated to God

and traveled out of the country for
the only time of His life.

As the boy Jesus
He
grew
became strong in Spirit
became strong in wisdom
He experienced His first Passover—
a great expectation ending in bewilderment.
Why?
All this confusion—buying and selling of a
marketplace.
Why?
All this bloody sacrifice—"My Father desires mercy,
not sacrifice."
Why?
No wisdom from the teachers who talk of Sabbath Law.
Why no mercy, love, and holiness?
His knowledge amazed the teachers
and puzzled the doctors
Mary and Joseph misunderstood Him
"Yet He was subject to them."

As Jesus the carpenter
He
humbled Himself with common man
toiled with a hammer and saw
shaped a yoke for oxen
possibly built a boat for Zebedee
learned the meaning of family life
learned to love God's world
watched children playing games
saw the sower sowing his seed
watched the corn ripen
saw the birds in the mustard tree
watched the beautiful poppies bloom
saw the good shepherds at work
watched Mary use leaven to make bread
helped in the frantic search for a lost coin

knew not to put new wine in old skins or not to put a
    new patch on an old garment
learned to pray

Knew—
the joy of a village wedding
the need of light
the value of salt
the sadness of a death
what it meant to be faithful over little,
And, as His custom was, He went into the synagogue
on the Sabbath Day.

It was during these hidden years
that Jesus was trusting the Father
He knew
why He was here
what was required of Him, and
who the suffering servant of Isaiah 53 was;
But Jesus waited patiently
for the call of the Father;
To be made Master over much
He must be faithful over little.
From the Jordan wilderness
the voice of John the Baptist cried
"Repent of your sins
Be baptized
Get ready
The King is coming."

The first to bear witness
was the last of the prophets
A lamp to point others to the Light
A voice to lead others to the Word
The lamp was only a spark
But the Light became a flame
The voice faded
But the Word abided.

As Jesus our King
He quickly
identified with sinful man

defeated the tempter
turned water into wine
cleansed the temple
healed the sick
stilled the storm
fed the five thousand
walked on the water
made the blind see
the lame walk
the broken whole
the crooked straight
the leper clean
the possessed free
the deaf to hear, and brought the dead to life
spoke with authority
blessed the humble
put down the hypocrites
taught by doing
walked over 2,500 miles
"that we might have life and
have it more abundantly."

His message—so easy
No matter how good you are—"Ye must"
No matter how bad you are—"You can"
"He that heareth . . . and believeth
. . . hath everlasting life."
His love—so great
"He gave us the gift of life
the blessing of love
Grace equal to every need
and peace like a dove."
Just believe and love
Love the Lord and
love your neighbor
as you love yourself.
But they had no love
"They saw no beauty in Him that they
might desire Him."

Who do men say that I am?

John the Baptist
Elijah
Jeremiah
The prophet
The carpenter
Rabbi
The prince of demons
The Nazarene, and
Good Master
We know that you are a teacher sent from God.
No, Nicodemus, God came to teach.

Peter—who do men say that I am?
"Thou art the Christ,
the son of the Living God."

Ask the world
To the
accused, He's the faithful witness
artist, He's altogether lovely
architect, He's the cornerstone
astronomer, He's the Bright and Morning Star
astronaut, He hangeth the earth upon nothing
attorney, He's the righteous judge
baker, He's the Bread of Life
banker, He's the Hidden Treasure
biologist, He's the Life
butler, He's the Good Master
carpenter, He's the door
doctor, He's the Great Physician
farmer, He's the Lord of the Harvest
florist, He's the Lily of the Valley
forester, He's the Tree of Life
geologist, He's the Rock of Ages
hunter, He's the Lion of Judah
jeweler, He's the Pearl of Great Price
musician, He's the Horn of Salvation
preacher, He's the Truth
publisher, He's the Author of our Salvation
sailor, He's the Light
soldier, He's the Leader and Commander

student, He's the Good Teacher
To mankind
He's the Lamb of God who taketh away the
sin of the world
To me
He is Lord.

He leads the world's greatest volunteer army
yet He refused to be a military leader.

He has healed more broken hearts
than doctors have healed broken bones,
yet he never practiced medicine.

He told us
to let our lights shine for God's glory
that those who hungered would be filled
to ask, seek, and knock
to have heavenly treasures
to forgive men their trespasses
to judge with great care
to trust in God
to freely give
to take His yoke upon us
His yoke fits well
and His burden is light
to have great faith
to ask in prayer
   according to His will
   in His name believing
to be merciful
to give God His due
to love our enemies
by the measure we give, we receive
to do as He has done
to take up His cross daily and follow Him
to not look back
to hear and keep the Word of God
to confess Him before men
to enter at the narrow gate
to whom much has been given

much will be required
to be faithful over small things
that it is more blessed to give
than to receive
to serve only one Master—the Lord
that without Him, we can do nothing
that He would not leave us comfortless
if we follow His commandments
we are His friend
to beware of false prophets
to watch and be ready for His return
that He would give us power and boldness
that we are to be His witnesses.

"Hosanna! Hosanna!
Blessed is the King of Israel, who cometh in the
name of the Lord."

Behold the betrayer is here with us.

"Father, if thou be willing, remove this cup from me,
nevertheless, not my will but thine be done."

"For this cause I came."

Judas betrayed Him,
the soldiers arrested Him,
bound Him, and
took Him to be judged.

He was falsely accused
but found without fault
and offered for release.

But where are the apostles?
Where are those He healed?
Where are those who praised Him?

The people cried
"Crucify Him."

The soldiers
scourged Him
stripped Him

171

dressed Him in scarlet robes
placed a crown of thorns on Him
mocked Him
led Him to Calvary
nailed Him to the cross and
crucified Him
parted His garments
casting lots for them.

He was
reviled by man
mocked by the chief priest
crucified between two thieves

Yet His words were not bitter, but
"Father, forgive them."
Reviled by the thieves
with one repenting
and our Master
forgave again.

Then darkness
The Father could look no longer
Jesus cried
Father, don't forsake me.

He lowered His head
and repeated a prayer taught to all
Jewish children,
"Father, into thine hands
I commit my Spirit."

While the passover lambs were being sacrificed
at the temple
The Lamb of God was being sacrificed
at Calvary.

Put Him in here
seal it with this stone
place a guard here.

Let's go to the tomb.
"He is not here, He is risen."

Herod could not kill Him
Satan could not seduce Him
Death could not destroy Him, the
Grave could not hold Him.

He gave up His heavenly robes
He became poor
that we might be rich.

How poor?
Ask
Mary
the shepherds
the wise men
For He
slept in another's manger
toured Lake Galilee in another's boat
ate in another's house
rode on another's donkey, and
was buried in another's tomb.

He did all this because He loves us.

How could He love us?
we desecrate His day
we steal His money
we blaspheme His name

Yet He still loves us.
He knows the number of the hairs on our heads.
He knows our thoughts before we think them—
And He still loves us.

He left His heavenly throne
came to earth
lived a perfect life
went to the old rugged cross
bled, died, and poured out
His life on Calvary
for every man, every woman,
for every boy, every girl,
for "whosoever will."

Tell me of Jesus?
The Father said it all,
"This is my beloved Son
In whom I am well pleased."